JOHN PAUL II
the great

WHITE STAR PUBLISHERS

Contents

Introduction	PAGE 12
The Vatican, The City, The State	PAGE 26
Private Life	PAGE 50
Papal Journeys	PAGE 72
The Last Farewell	PAGE 202

Photographs
Gianni Giansanti

Text
Marco Tosatti

Design
Patrizia Balocco Lovisetti

This book was produced with the help of the press office of the Holy See.

© 2005 White Star S.p.a.
Via Candido Sassone, 22/24
13100 Vercelli, Italia
www.whitestar.it

Translation: Jane Glover and Studio Traduzione Vecchia

All rights reserved. No part of this publication may be reproduced, stored in a retrieval system or transmitted in any form or by any means, electronic, mechanical, photocopying, recording or otherwise, without written permission from the publisher.
White Star Publishers® is a registered trademark property of Edizioni White Star.
ISBN 88-544-0104-8
REPRINTS:
1 2 3 4 5 6   09 08 07 06 05
Printed in Spagna

1 *One of the most celebrated ceremonies: the Palm Sunday celebration in St. Peter's Square.*

2-3 *John Paul II caught in one of his most characteristic poses: after giving the closing blessing at the end of the ceremony he greets the pilgrims with his arms raised, a gesture which has nothing to do with accepted papal protocol, but one which never fails to delight the crowds.*

4-5 *A solemn mass is celebrated in the Sistine Chapel. Sixtus IV summoned Michelangelo to start the fresco cycle on the vault in 1508; some years later the artist's Last Judgement concluded the magnificent work.*

6-7 *The Hill of Crosses, Lithuania, 1993:*
"*To commemorate the sons and the daughters of your land, those who were tried, those who were imprisoned, sent to concentration camps, deported to Siberia, condemned to death.*" *Although partially destroyed several times, the Hill of Crosses has always been rebuilt.*

8-9 *Krakow, 1983. Poland after the Jaruzelski coup:*
"*I ask you to call these weaknesses, these sins, these vices, these situations, by their names. To fight them without ceasing.*"

10-11 *Vatican City, April 8th, 2005. Cardinals, bishops, heads of state, kings and queens attend the funeral mass for Pope John Paul II. Karol Wojtyla's body lay in a simple cedar coffin, placed on a damask carpet. The Gospels were placed on the lid of the coffin.*

12-13 *Panama, April 1987. The Pope in a moment of spiritual isolation during the reading of the Gospel.*

13 (top) *October 16, 1978. On the day he was elected, John Paul II spoke with humility: "If I make mistakes . . . if I make mistakes you will correct me."*

INTRODUCTION

History suggests that St. Peter, first bishop of Rome, led the Church for twenty-five years before his crucifixion in about A.D. 64. Almost two thousand years later, Pope John Paul II, who might well be named Courage, led the Church into the doors to the 21st century, his vision and thoughts turned toward the year 2000. He was a wearied Moses in the last period of his life, worn out by the road. He guided his flock, a people that was a little resistant at times, a little distracted at times by an excess of temptations, to round the cape into the third millennium. Some time ago he admitted he was old and started making jokes about his health; then he stopped that, and instead he began to try and conserve the energy he began to lack, like a traveler intent on reaching his destination at all costs, conscious that he cannot waste his remaining strength. Tired, but determined not to give up. "I renew before Christ," he said, in a general policy manifesto, "the pledge of my willingness to serve the Church for as long as He wants me to, abandoning myself entirely to His holy will. I leave to Him the decision as to how he will relieve me of this service."

Of course, for Karol Wojtyla the climb became harder and harder. In the past, in the prime of his life and enthusiasm, he would throw children up into the air then catch them and give them back to their proud and amazed parents. But as the years passed he stopped at a pat, a kiss on the head. And although we sometimes saw him clutching – or perhaps even brandishing – his pastoral staff in his final years, before sickness forced him to use the mobile platform, that staff, which was the sign of his power – and his duty – was needed more as a support than to threaten chastisement. He was quite right to want to rest a little, this man who was physically worn-out by a life lived to the full. Everyone remembers the near-fatal assassination attempt of 13 May 1981 (John Paul II was convinced that the Virgin Mary intervened on that occasion). In 1992 he had a long stay – sixteen days – in the Gemelli Hospital, after an operation to remove a tumor. Then, the incident during his address to the Food and Agriculture Organization (FAO), in

November 1993, when he broke a small bone in his shoulder, forced him to have a cumbersome plaster cast. A decisive moment came when he fell in the bath in April 1994, leading to yet another trip to the Gemelli Hospital, whose papal suite was always ready to receive Christ's Vicar on earth; this time he had a femoral prosthesis fitted to his right leg. He started to walk again; but the operation was not a success, and problems with his leg, especially the knee, meant he was forced to stay immobile. These painful setbacks were made worse in 1992 by Parkinson's disease, although the first symptoms may have appeared earlier. In addition to this, according to the Vatican, he had some back problems which dated to his time in the war and which he uncomplainingly and courageously put up with over the years. Indeed, he had every good reason to wish for a quieter existence, especially in the autumn and the harsh winter of his life.

But Pope John Paul II had other things on his mind. "We will have the whole of eternity to rest," he had replied a few years ago, after he returned from a particularly wearing trip and somebody pointed out that his schedule for the next day was already full of tiring commitments. Again, this seems to be the key to understanding the deep "animus" of the late Pope, "Karol the Great"; this is the thread that embroiders the story, at times incredible with something of a 20th-century fable, of this boy from the Polish provinces who became the most famous man, the definitive global "personality" bestriding the end of the last century.

No Pope, and perhaps no man in history, had been so photographed, filmed, broadcast, had held the global mass-media stage with such strength and determination. This man lived through four eras and entered the fifth, an unknown ocean, leading the Church into the Third Millennium. He knew the rural Poland of the period immediately following the First World War, the Industrial Revolution and the drama of the war with Nazi Germany, the Communist regime, which was expected to last for a thousand years, and then the sudden, dramatic collapse of the Eastern bloc of Communist countries, with its legacy of unsolved problems, smashed hopes, social and human disorder.

14-15 *General audience in the Nervi Hall.
The hall is named after the architect who designed it.
A sculpture of Christ by the Italian artist Pericle
Fazzini dominates the background.*

16-17 *Another of Pope John Paul II's regular appointments: the Sunday Angelus from the window of his study in St. Peter's Square. The Angelus is usually an opportunity to comment on current events of a particularly interesting or serious nature.*

Karol Wojtyla was born in Wadowice, a small town in Poland, on 18 May 1920, to Jozef and Emilia Kaczorowscy. His father was a professional soldier pensioned off early due to poor health. When "Lolek" was only nine years old, his mother died from a kidney infection. The shadow of premature death was to leave a heavy mark on Lolek's life – a sister had died at a very early age, before he was born, and later, in 1938, a scarlet fever epidemic cost him his elder brother, a doctor at Bielsko Biala on the Czechoslovak border. He moved to Kraków with his father to continue his education, but a year later, on 1 September 1939, Hitler invaded Poland. Five days later Nazi troops entered Kraków, and, in order to avoid deportation or the concentration camps, along with many other young Poles Karol found work on the factory floor, in his case, with the Solvay company. This is how the himself describes his experience, in his book *The Nest I Came From*: "In September 1940 I started work in the Zakrzowek stone quarry. In the summer of 1941 I moved into the factory, working on the water purifying plant for the boiler room. After the accident in 1944 [the future Pope was knocked down by a German truck] I was moved to the carbonated division. I left work at the beginning of August 1944 to take up my studies again in the third year of the metropolitan seminary." In the meantime his father had also died, of a heart attack.

These were the crucial years in which the young Krakovian student with a passion for drama, both as actor and author, and for writing poetry (under the pen name of Andrzej Jawien) metamorphosed into the future priest and bishop. These were also the years when, some say, the young Karol was brushed by the scent of an earthly love, of a mysterious woman who appeared in his life before he entered the clandestine seminary in Kraków. His friend and biographer, Mieczyslaw Malinski, dismisses the rumor with a laugh. The story of a young woman who was killed and her lover from Wadowice who decided to turn to the priesthood is indeed a true one; it does not, however, involve Karol Wojtyla but another Polish prelate, Monsignor Kuczkowski.

18-19 *Before the assassination attempt it was quite normal to see the Pope's white jeep among the crowds in St. Peter's Square.*

During his time in the factory Lolek studied and prayed. One of his companions at that time has this to say: "At around midnight during the night shift, he used to kneel down and pray right in the middle of the shop-floor ... not all the workers there showed respect for his devotion. Some of them used to chuck rags or other things at him, to distract him."

But he had already made his final choice: on November 1, 1946, Karol Wojtyla was ordained into the priesthood by the celebrated Archbishop of Kraków, Cardinal Sapieha.

After the agony of the Nazi madness, the world moved into an era known as the Cold War

19 (top) *The ejected bullet case lying on the cobbles in the basilica courtyard bears witness to the drama that has just taken place: the attempt on the Pope's life.*

19 (bottom) *Roses that a pilgrim had intended to hand to the Pope are left on the steps next to the empty chair.*

and dominated by two groupings of states. New and unimagined horizons were opening up to the young boy from Wadowice. It was the start of the *cursus honorum* that would lead him to Rome, first as a theology student at the Dominican Angelicum College, and then into a rapid crescendo of appointments. He taught philosophy at Lublin University and was appointed bishop and then auxiliary at Kraków. He took an active part in the Second Vatican Council, and on 18 January 1964, Pope Paul VI appointed him Archbishop of Kraków.

Karol Wojtyla has been called the world's parish priest. It is an apt title, even though it encapsulates only one of the facets of his personality, and it was in the 1960s that the future Pope laid the foundations of his great pastoral and political activity in Poland. The boys at St. Florian's, Kraków, where he was just a lowly priest, called him "Uncle," and so did the girls at St. Anne's parish, whom he used to take walking in the mountains around Zakopane. His was a direct, uncomplicated relationship with the faithful, accompanied by intense involvement in cultural activities to combat the Communist regime. He founded the Institute for the Family, gave help to a political movement called ZNAK, which adopted a critical stance toward the government, and worked hard to get the theological faculty set up. Those were the years of the celebrated battle of Nova Huta, when the government blocked the attempt to build a new church in this industrial satellite town. The harshest period of the battle would occur when Solidarity, the free trade union founded in 1980, lent its support to the fight. But by that time Wojtyla had already gone to the Vatican in Rome; the battle finally ended in 1989, with the collapse of the Communist regimes in central and eastern Europe.

In 1967 forty-seven-year-old Karol Wojtyla was the youngest cardinal in the Roman Catholic Church, but it was already some years since Lolek had first crossed the borders of Krakow and Poland to visit the Polish communities spread around the world, as far away as Papua New Guinea. Traveling is another aspect of the *cursus honorum* and an indispensable part of achieving high office in the church. It is a way of becoming well known, of establishing direct relations with local churches, and of discovering the facts and diverse requirements of particular situations and problems light years away from each other. Pope John Paul II would visit very few countries that Archbishop or Cardinal Wojtyla had not already seen. The strange tale of the little boy from Wadowice ended – or was it just beginning? – on 16 October 1978 in St. Peter's Square, with the words "If I make mistakes … if I make mistakes, you will correct me." He was the first Slav Pope in history, the first non-Italian since Hadrian VI of Utrecht, who was elected in 1522 and died in 1523. Since that October day nearly twenty-seven years of eventful history have passed: the first visit to the Rome synagogue; the friendship with Alessandro Pertini, then president of Italy; Solidarity and the confrontation with General Jaruszelski; the prayer meeting for peace with all the world's religions at Assisi; the "rehabilitation" of Galileo; the collapse of the "Evil Empire"; fourteen encyclicals, eight apostolic exhortations, ten apostolic "Constitutions," thirty-seven apostolic letters, not to mention a tidal wave of discourses. He has called ten synods and nine consistories. He proclaimed more than 1300 saints and members of the Blessed.

"He is still alive," he jokingly replied to young people who greeted him with cries of "Long live the Pope," and on the flight to the United States at the end of 1995 he said, "You can see for yourselves, I am well, the Pope is still alive." He was tired, a little worn, fighting Parkinson's disease, which had so cruelly struck him down in what had always been his forte, his expressiveness. And yet he has had the immense joy of opening the Holy Door of St. Peter's to the Jubilee of the Second Millennium. Or rather, the Holy Doors, because he also wanted to open wide the portals of the other great Roman churches, San Giovanni, Santa Maria Maggiore, and San Paolo fuori le Mura. He has realized many of his dreams: he has visited Cuba, been to Lebanon, and has retraced the footsteps of Moses in the Sinai and Cairo. And he was only the second Pope in history, after Paul VI, to go to the Holy Land on an unprecedented trip that included Jordan, Israel, and Palestine. Moscow and China were all that remained. Limping (and later on sitting on his mobile chair) he has walked on and on. Like the Polish hymn: "March, march Dabrowski, from the soil of Italy…"

20 *Vatican City, 24 December 1999.*
John Paul II halts to pray at the entrance to the Basilica of St. Peter soon after having opened the Holy Gate in the official beginning of the Jubilee Year.

22-23 *A general audience in St. Peter's Square: the Pope's hand and the pilgrims' hands.*

24-25 *Two children greet the Pope in Baltimore in October 1995.*

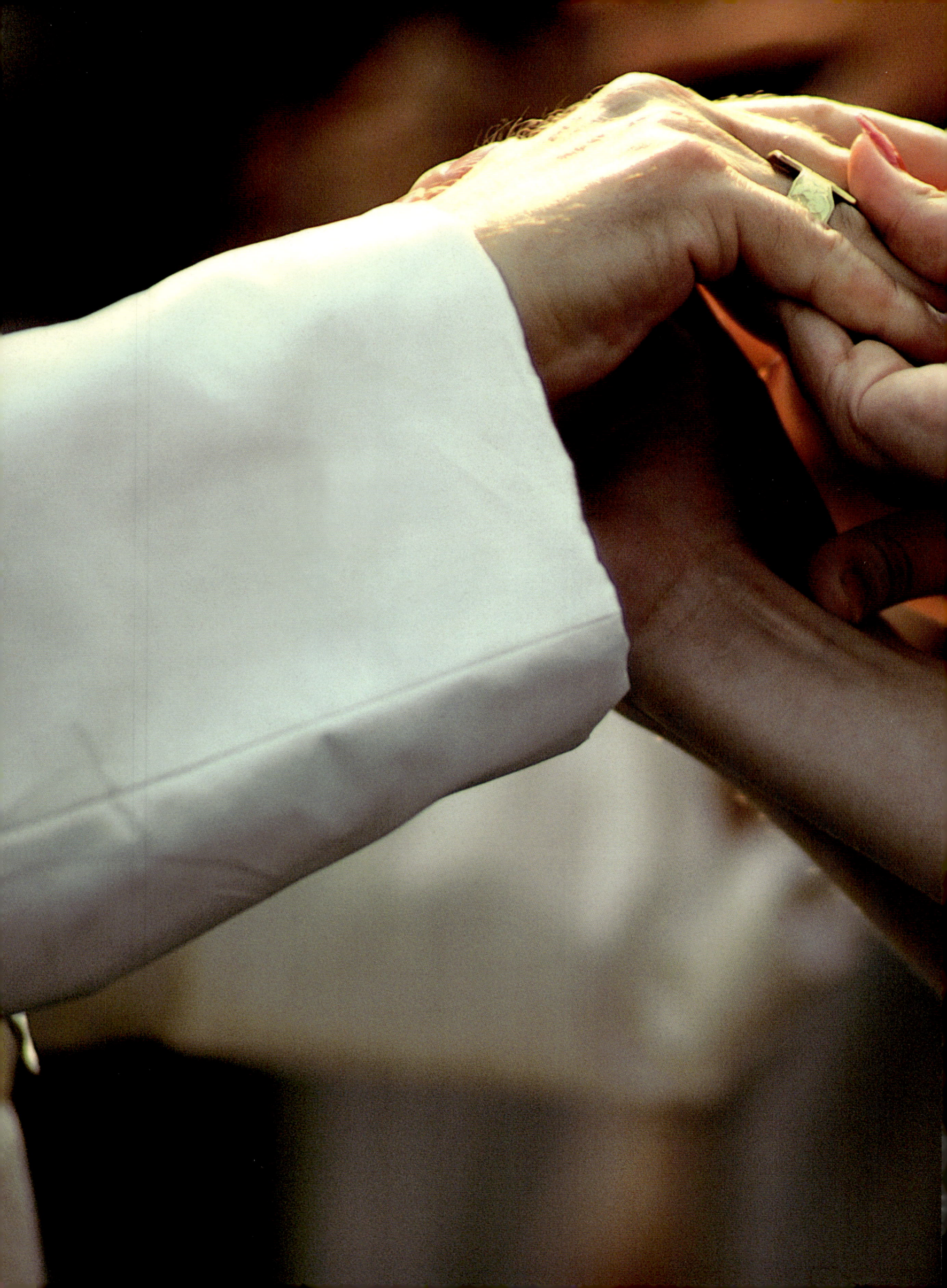

The Vatican, The City, The State

26-27 *From the liturgical point of view the beatification ceremony is one of the pontificate's most spectacular moments, particularly when it takes place in Christianity's "head" church. The photograph is of the beatification of Monsignor Escrivà de Balaguer, in May 1992.*

29 *The imposing* The Last Judgment, *painted by Michelangelo between 1436 and 1441, shines out brightly in its restored colors, behind John Paul II who is sitting on the central chair. The Sistine Chapel, as well as being the seat of the Conclave, was also the location for other solemn functions conducted by the Pope.*

The Vatican is first and foremost a tomb; indeed, it is *the* tomb – the tomb of the first Pope and Prince of the Apostles. According to tradition, Peter was crucified there during a particularly ferocious persecution of the early Christians. He chose to be executed upside down as a sign of humility toward Christ, who died with his eyes raised toward heaven. He was buried there, some eighteen feet below the basilica's high altar, the splendid bronze construction created by Bernini. The altar is known as the Altar of the Confession because that is where the old fisherman confessed his faith in Jesus Christ and underwent martyrdom.

Tradition was reinforced by papal authority. In 1968, when Paul VI gave official confirmation that one of the burials excavated in the grottoes underneath the basilica was that of the first Pope and had Peter's relics placed in the niche in nineteen Plexiglas containers. So the Vatican was founded upon a burial stone, at the time of Emperor Constantine, the first basilica being built in honor of Peter – and the other martyrs who shared his fate on the hill – conferring a unique charisma on the most important Roman Catholic basilica in the world. The memory of the Prince of the Apostles is everywhere in the church: "Tu es Petrus . . . thou art Peter and upon this rock I will build my church." The evangelical formula runs in large capital letters along the base of the cornice, above the drum of the dome. In the nave stands the bronze 13th-century statue of St. Peter, so greatly venerated that the right foot is worn from pilgrims' countless kisses and touches. Bernini's *Gloria* in the apse incorporates *St. Peter's Throne*, an extraordinary work decorated with ivory, and a gift of Charles the Bald made to Pope John VII in 706.

The Vatican and St. Peter's are the roots, the tangible, physical symbols wrought in stone and marble and bronze, of the Church's spiritual power. They form a mosaic that is steeped in history, tradition, faith, and politics. It is the only complex of its kind in the world, similar to but greater than other sacred sites: the Ka'aba at Mecca, the Temple site and West (Wailing) Wall in Jerusalem, the Ganges at Benares. A hill which was surrounded by marshes and fields in Roman times, the *ager vaticanus*, a name of Etruscan origin perhaps, is now probably one of the places with the highest density of works of art and history in the world, as well as a city, a state, and the seat of government of one of the most influential and widespread religions on the planet.

The first walls and towers were built on the hill by Pope Leo IV, round Constantine's basilica, in the 9th century, in part to defend against the Saracen raiders who were bold enough to sail up the Tiber. In the 12th century, Pope Innocent II added an inner ring of walls. In the 13th century, Pope Nicholas III, an Orsini, started building a two-story palace, the kernel of successive extensions and buildings from the Renaissance right up to the present, with St. Peter's as its center, the richest and most grandiose Roman Catholic church in the world. It is not John Paul II's episcopal seat (St. John Lateran is), nor is it his "parish" (this is St. Anne of the Palfreniers, next to Porta Angelica), but it represents the *sancta sanctorum* of the Roman Catholic Church. It is here, on the basilica's central balcony, that the new Pope makes his appearance on leaving the conclave by which he has just been elected; he gives most important messages, *Urbi et Orbi*, to the city and to the world, from the central loggia. On his return from every apostolic journey he goes to pray on St. Peter's tomb, and once a year he hears confession, just like any ordinary priest.

30-31 *Writing of Michelangelo, whom he calls "one of the Titans of art," Victor Hugo says that the artist "superimposed the Pantheon on the Parthenon and created St. Peter's." Despite the basilica's colossal size — 430 feet high by 613 feet long — critics stress that the harmony of its proportions restores the monument to a "human" scale.*

32-33 *The culminating moment during the ordination of eleven new bishops by the Pope in St. Peter's basilica.*

The Pope takes his legitimization and his power from Peter's tomb: he is the Bishop of Rome, the Vicar of Jesus Christ on Earth, the Successor of the Prince of the Apostles, the Pontifex Maximus of the universal Church, the Patriarch of the West, Primate of all Italy, Archbishop and Metropolitan of the Roman Province, Sovereign of the Vatican State and City. "Holy Father" or "Holiness" are the most direct and colloquial names for this man who rules over just 108 acres packed with buildings, more than fifty-five thousand square yards of them. Gardens, twenty or so courtyards, and around one thousand rooms of all sizes contain innumerable quantities of precious art objects, furniture, books, paintings, and manuscripts.

Not everything inside the walls has been catalogued or described. This is particularly true of some sections of the Vatican Library, where this work is currently being undertaken. It is because of this incredible density that Article 24 of the Lateran Treaty (1929) declares the tiny state as neutral in perpetuity and inviolable. Any hostile action, however limited, could produce irreparable damage. The Vatican was spared during Allied bombing raids on Rome during the Second World War, although one night an unidentified aircraft dropped some small-caliber bombs which caused insignificant damage.

The mystery has never been cleared up, for although the device had been made in Great Britain, a deliberate provocation could not be ruled out. Since 1954 the entire Vatican has been protected under the Hague Convention, and in 1984 the Vatican City was formally declared part of the World Art Heritage. However, in 1984 a bunker below the Cortile del Belvedere was officially opened to store the precious codices, manuscripts, and documents belonging to the Library and the Archives.

The border between Italy and the Vatican is invisible. It runs from the end of Via della Conciliazione at St. Peter's Square, where the third arm of Bernini's colonnade (had it been built) would have closed in the immense 70,000-

square-yard space that can hold 300,000 people. The Vatican State is miniscule, but like an enormous dime store, it houses the most disparate of objects: a functioning railway station and the *Osservatore Romano* (the Vatican newspaper); the Post and Telegraph building and a heliport; the polyglot Vatican Press and the Pharmacy; the Swiss Guards' barracks and arsenal and the Mosaic School. Then there is St. Martha's Hospice, a residential complex for visiting prelates and nuncios (following the Costituzione Apostolica Dominici Gregis, signed by John Paul II himself, the Hospice now hosts the cardinals gathered in conclave); the tapestry restoration workshops and the first headquarters of the Vatican Radio; the Papal Academy of Sciences, gardens, vegetable plots – fresh vegetables for the Pope's table as well as honey from the papal hives – and the Ethiopian College; the Tower of the Winds, Nervi Hall, and the Palace of the Holy Office. This does not include the museums and the papal palaces, the true nerve center of the universal Church.

The Pope is ruler of all this and much more besides, and his rule is absolute. In form at least, he is the last absolute sovereign left in the world, as absolute as the Louis XIV (the "Sun King") or Philip II of Spain, more so than Elizabeth I of England. The Constitutional Law promulgated on June 7, 1929, and still in force, gives the Pope all legislative, executive, and judicial power. His person unites everything that modern states divide among the executive, legislative and judiciary branches. He is a sovereign by divine, not elective, right, drawing his power from God Himself. The conclave is only a system to designate him; the electing cardinals do not transfer any of their power to him, they are simply the Holy Spirit's tool.

From the papal palaces the Pope guides and controls three parallel structures. The first, and smallest, of these is the Vatican City, the miniscule relic of temporal power which is guaranteed to the pontiff so that he can exercise his moral and pastoral power in total freedom,

34-35 *The washing of the feet is one of the most significant of the Easter ceremonies. Here John Paul II is seen taking part in the ritual in the basilica of St. John Lateran.*

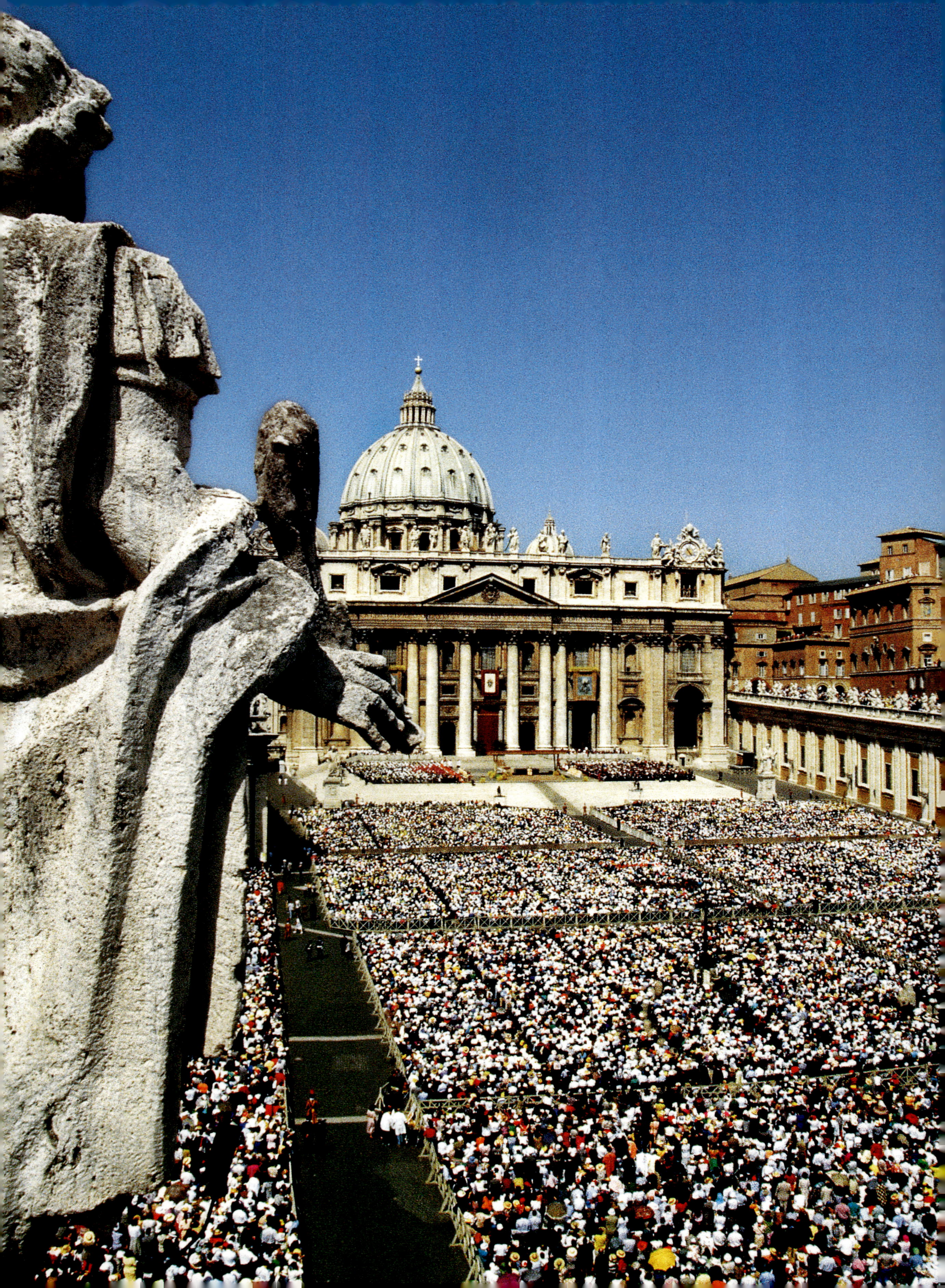

36 *St. Peter's Square provides the visitor with the greatest of all Baroque scenarios. The immense court covers 70,000 square yards, one-sixth of the total area of the Vatican. It is indeed the foreground to St. Peter's basilica, the ideal stage for the Church's great liturgies.*

without being influenced by any state. Then there is the Holy See (i.e., the international organ which accredits ambassadors and appoints papal nuncios, and which has differing levels of diplomatic relations with some 120 nations throughout the world), the Pope's official and diplomatic face. Finally there is the Universal Church, closely linked from an operational standpoint with the Holy See, but not automatically identifiable with it. It is a complex arrangement where many of the possible problems and demarcation conflicts are resolved due to their common dependence on the Pope's absolute authority.

The Church's first task is to defend and to spread the Roman Catholic doctrine, and the Vatican has, over the years, supplied itself with the necessary tools. Thus there is a Congregation for the Doctrine of the Faith (previously the Holy Office), whose function is to ensure that bishops, theologians, and priests do not express any opinions contradicting the consolidated doctrine of the faith and to punish those who do. There are over four thousand bishops in the Roman Catholic Church, and a Congregation is needed to oversee their nominations, transfers, and everything else concerning this sensitive sector. The Congregation for Clerics has the same function with respect to priests, while the role of the Congregation for Monastics is to supervise the many Sacred Orders; these orders are in fact allowed considerable autonomy (which they guard jealously), the only exception being the Jesuits, who are bound to the Pope by a vow of total obedience: *perinde ac cadaver*. The very powerful Congregation for the Propagation of the Faith (its prefect is known as the Red Pope, while the General of the Company of Jesus is called the Black Pope) keeps a watch over the missionary churches, especially in Africa.

At the head of the whole organization is the Secretariat of State, which flanks the Pope – in the physical sense too, as the offices are in the apostolic palaces. This is the Holy See's political organ. It has a Secretary of State, whose position could be compared to that of a head of government. One section of the Secretariat acts as a Ministry of Foreign Affairs and is divided into linguistic sections. It plays a very important role in the general life of the Church, particularly in the preparation of the Pope's trips and the writing of his speeches. Before the Parkinson's disease left him almost without speech, the Pope made dozens, if not hundreds, of major addresses each year. The Secretary of State also coordinates the work of the nuncios, the Pope's ambassadors, throughout the world.

Around twenty-three hundred people work in the Vatican: thirteen hundred lay people, including around three hundred women, and eight hundred priests or members of religious orders. In the past few decades the Curia, including the College of Cardinals, has experienced an accelerated rate of internationalization, and the reign of the Slav Pope has naturally accentuated this trend. Very few of these employees live within the walls, and there are only a small number – not counting the diplomats – who carry a passport issued by the Holy See.

Life inside the Vatican City is bustling in the morning, when the coming and going through Porta S. Anna (St. Anne's Gate) is quite intense. The Swiss Guards and the Vatican's security service have their work cut out keeping watch over the "border" crossing. In the afternoon the city seems to slip little by little into a torpor, until the moment late in the evening when only the Swiss remain to guard the gate. A reminder of times long passed, they are the only picturesque element remaining from earlier times and other Pontiffs. It was Julius II, the terrible Della Rovere Pope, who recruited the first Swiss in 1505 for use in the Italian wars. The Swiss Guards are all that remain of the many pontifical guards (including a little-known Corsican Guard in the 17th century) down the centuries. Famous for their loyalty – in 1527 they sacrificed themselves in combat with the Constable of Bourbon's lansquenets, in order that Clement VII might escape to Castel Sant-Angelo by the Passetto di Borgo – they are all volunteers. The majority are recruited from the

German-speaking Swiss cantons, signing on for two-year contracts; they live, for two years at least, in the barracks at the Porta S. Anna entrance. Wearing their blue-and-orange-striped uniforms, with puffed sleeves and big hats, or breastplates and morions, armed with halberd and sword, they are the delight of camera-wielding tourists.

Everything about this state is different, especially as far as its finances are concerned. Is the Church poor? It seems incredible, but it is to some extent true, and the Holy See, the central office of Roman Catholicism, is particularly in need. The Vatican City (i.e., the physical part of the state) has its own budget and makes a profit thanks to the museums. The Holy See, or rather the ministries, the Secretariat, the Vatican Radio, and *Osservatore Romano*, in addition to the nunciatures around the world, cost around $158 million annually. The only income to cover the costs of central government is from the rents collected on real estate, the yield from the "dowry" bestowed by the Italian state in 1929, and the offertories from the dioceses all over the world. The biggest contributors are the U.S. bishops, followed by the Germans, and for some years now, the Italians, thanks perhaps to a miniscule levy on income tax. The payroll is the largest item of expenditure (ca. $67 million). The Vatican Library and Press cost around $18 million, but produce a small profit. The Vatican Radio and *Osservatore Romano*, on the other hand, produce no dividends other than the spiritual kind and cost around $4 million and $19 million respectively. The "Voice of the Pope" broadcasts regularly in forty different languages, including Arabic, Chinese, Aramaic, and Swahili.

38-39 *The Swiss Guards, pictured here on sentry duty at the Bell Arch (one of the entrances to the Vatican next to St. Peter's), are one of the more fascinating aspects of Vatican folklore. A large part of their charm is due to the blue-and-orange-striped uniform, perhaps designed by Michelangelo, and their Renaissance swords and halberds.*

PAVLVS·V·PONT·MAX·ANNO·XIIII
PAVLVS VI PONT MAX
HVIVS PATRIARCALIS
VATICANAE BASILICAE
PORTAM SANCTAM
APERVIT ET CLAVSIT
ANNO IVBILAEI MCMLXXV
PIVS XII PONT MAX
PORTAM SANCTAM
A PIO XI PONT MAX
ANNO IVBILAEI
MCMXXXIII XXXIV
RESERATAM ET CLAVSAM
APERVIT ET CLAVSIT
ANNO IVBILAEI MCML

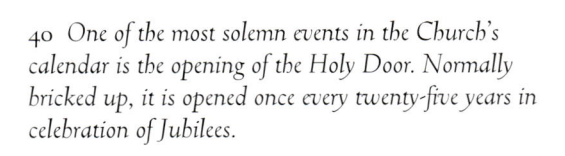

40 One of the most solemn events in the Church's calendar is the opening of the Holy Door. Normally bricked up, it is opened once every twenty-five years in celebration of Jubilees.

41 The Pope, immediately after entering the basilica through the Holy Door, at the start of the extraordinary Jubilee in 1983.

42 *The Pope seated beneath Bernini's canopy at the Altar of the Confession. Bernini drew the inspiration for his twisted columns from an Egyptian column long held inside the basilica.*

43 *John Paul II enthroned during a solemn ceremony in the true heart of Christianity, that part of the Vatican basilica constructed over St. Peter's tomb. Behind him is the St. Helena, the best-known work of Andrea Bolgi, a pupil of Bernini.*

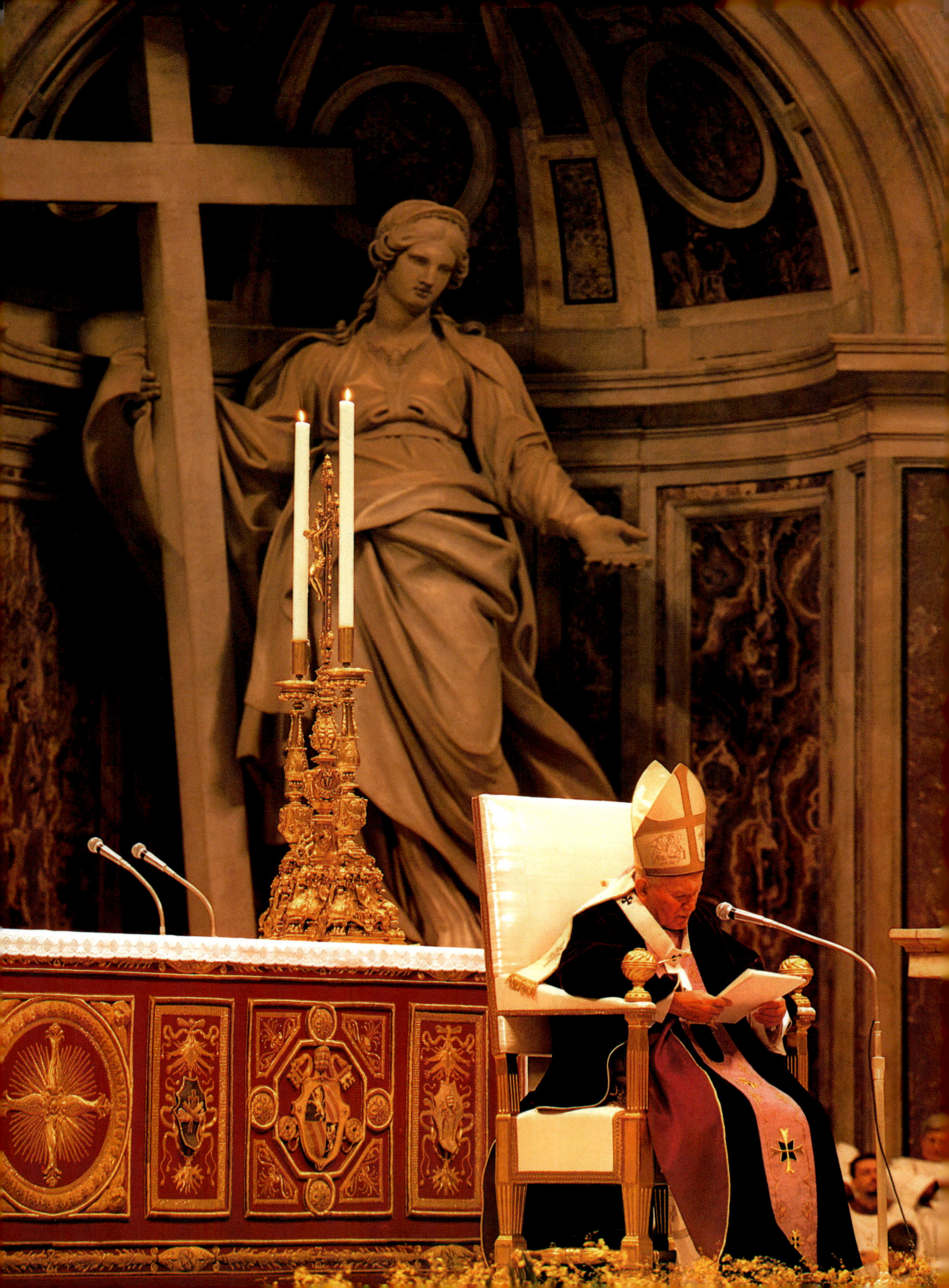

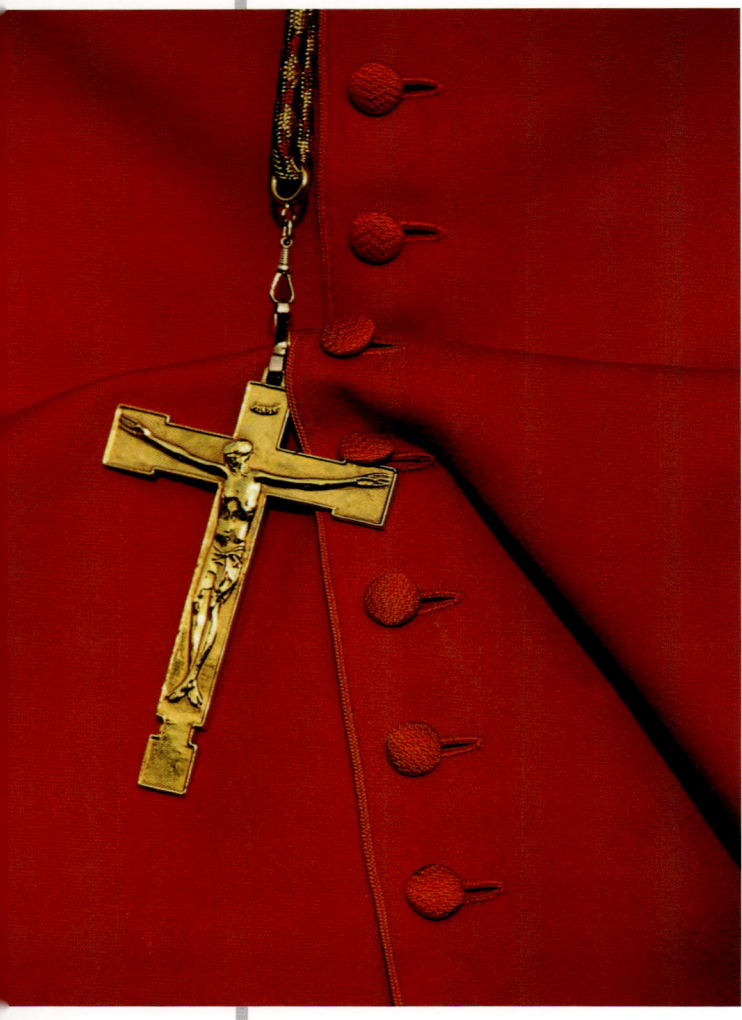

44 Faith feeds upon symbols and images. The gold cardinal's cross is the symbol of the "Princes of the Church," men chosen to constitute the Senate of Catholicity and the potential electorate of Popes. Red, a "noble" color in many cultures, is especially significant in Roman Catholic symbology since bishops and cardinals must witness to the faith *usque ad sanguinem* — as far as martyrdom.

44-45 *John Paul II places the cardinal's berretta on the head of the Bishop of Sarajevo, Monsignor Vinko Puljic, in November 1994.*

46-47 *A photograph of His Holiness during the Family Synod in 1994 catches him in a tired moment, but the arrival of a child with a candle for the Pope is all that is necessary to revive him.*

48-49 *John Paul II has never missed the Via Crucis in the Coliseum. At Easter 1995, despite his obvious difficulty in walking after a hip operation, he insisted on completing the stations and even holding, briefly, the heavy cross at the head of the procession.*

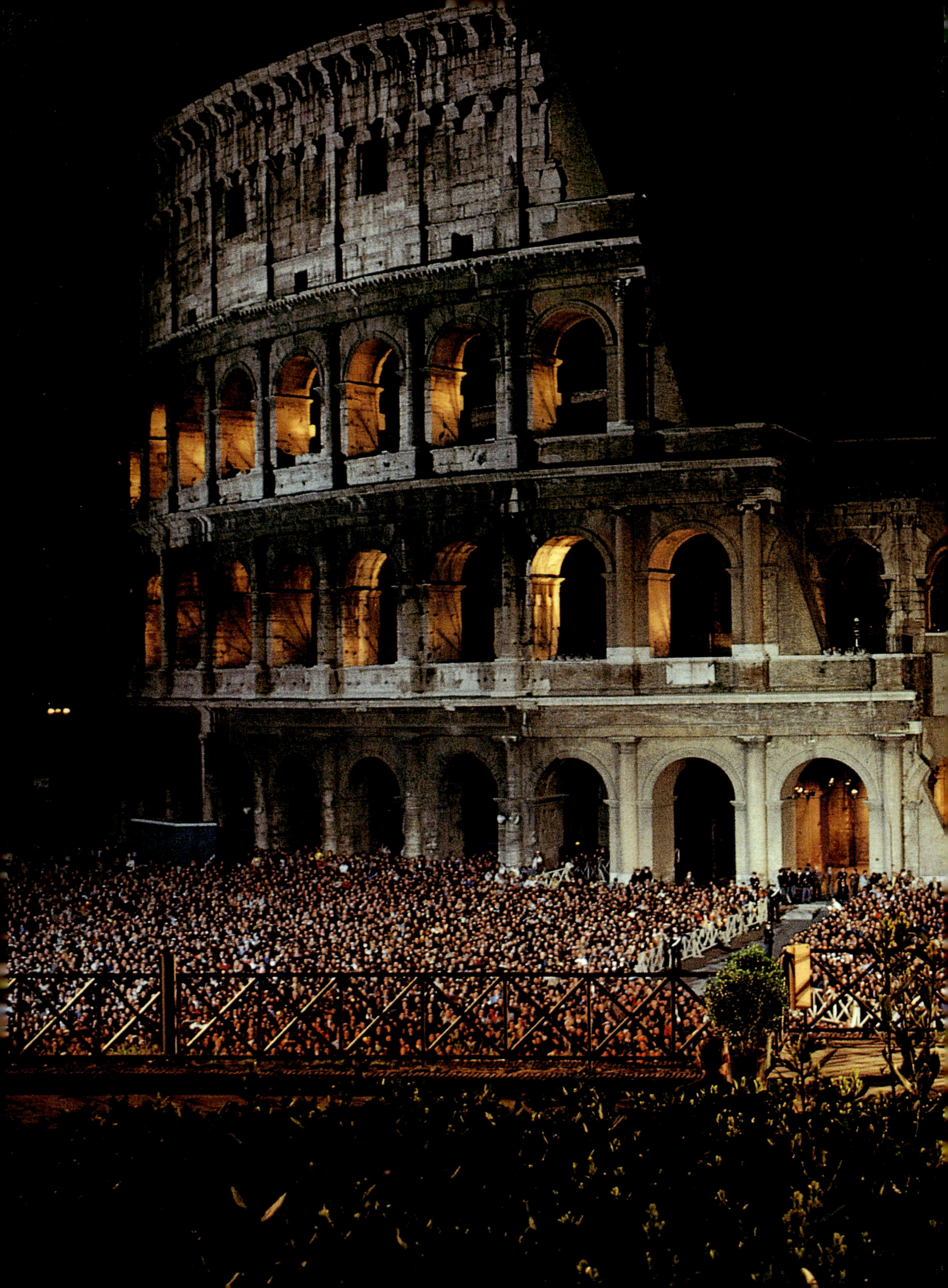

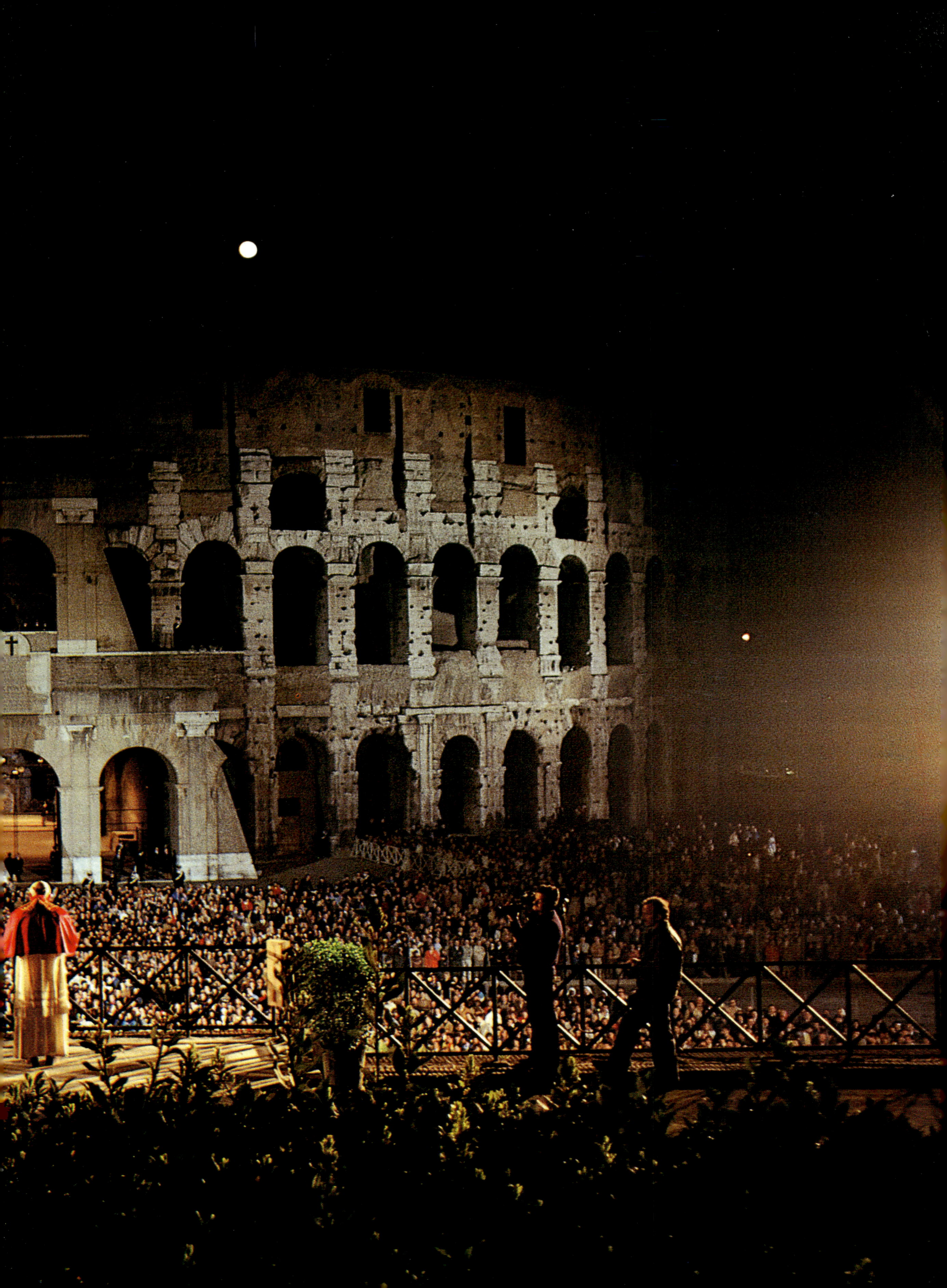

Private Life

*S*olitude is the burden of every Pope and especially affected John Paul II. It is a solitude packed with people, busy with engagements and crowds, but this does not make it any lighter, or any less continuous or threatening. The solitude of a Pope is that of a man burdened with an enormous responsibility, a weight that caused Paul VI to suffer and that crushed John Paul I. It is the solitude of a helmsman steering a ship that is not his own – the Church – in a world like "the dark night of the soul" that Karol Wojtyla's favorite mystic, Giovanni Della Croce, wrote about. "The Pope is the most solitary man in the world" has been a truism in the Vatican for decades. But John Paul II used to fill this definition with his own particular style. His was the solitude of a mystic, of a man continually searching for the final Being. His is a special kind of solitude, closely connected to his way of praying and of working. When he was Archbishop of Kraków, writes Mieczyslaw Malinski in *My Old Friend Karol*, the first biography of Wojtyla as Pope, "he used to pray in that characteristic stance of his, leaning forward, his head resting on one hand, the palm covering his face, or with his head resting on both hands. He used to stay in the same position for long periods at a time." And like many solitary travelers of the road which leads to the absolute, his prayer took extreme forms: "He would sometimes lie prostrate in the shape of the cross" on the floor in front of the altar. "His driver told me, after he had entered the chapel by mistake once."

In Kraków, Wojtyla would write, read, and pray in the chapel. In the Vatican the chapel was his first commitment every day. When he was still in good health, the Pope used to rise, not very willingly, at around 5:30 a.m.

50-51 *The Pontiff signing a document in the Library. This is the room where John Paul II, like Paul VI before him, has met and talked with the powerful of the earth: Gorbachev, Reagan, Clinton, and Yeltsin have all sat at this table.*

52-53 *Every morning John Paul II spends time in silent meditation in the private chapel, while a nun prepares the altar for morning mass.*

54-55 *John Paul II at prayer in his private chapel, while in the background guests wait to take part in the morning celebration of mass.*

Apparently he has never liked early starts. Paul VI had some exercise equipment installed in the private apartments and John Paul II has continued to use it, adding some specific rehabilitation apparatus – a harsh necessity after his accidents. Then he went to chapel to pray and meditate. The chapel, which was refurbished under Paul VI, is not very big. There are two bronze doors by Enrico Manfrini, illustrating episodes from the life of Christ. A single column holds the most simple of altars in white marble. In the background is the Martyrdom of Saints Peter and Paul. The bright, stained-glass ceiling is the work of Luigi Filocamo. A host of angels surrounds the risen Christ in glory. At exactly 7.00 o'clock, John Paul II celebrated mass. Every day the nuns of the Sisters of the Sacred Heart Order of Kraków, who looked after the Pope's housekeeping and cooking, and his private secretary Monsignor Stanislaw Dziwisz, a discreet and attentive figure who has been in the Pope's service since Kraków, attended this mass. In the last years, another secretary from Poland, Don Mietek, took the place of Monsignor Stanislaw – who, in the meantime, has become cardinal – in the management of everyday care on Pope's needs – a difficult task.

Sometimes there were guests. A few days beforehand, each of the fortunate invitees received a telephone call from Monsignor Stanislaw: "This is the Pope's private secretary. Would you please be at the Bronze Gate at 5:30 a.m.?" The Pope used to celebrate mass slowly, in Latin, Italian, or Polish, but the language chosen for the liturgy might depend upon the nationality of the guests, a particularly courteous gesture. It was always an intense celebration; the Pope allowed a long time for the prayers of preparation and the giving of thanks after the Eucharist. At the end he greeted his guests in the nearby Library, saying a few words to each of them while the official photographer took the ritual snaps.

Breakfast came after mass, either with guests or just people from the household. The table was a simple rectangle, with ten chairs at the most, all identical, with the same high backs and arms.

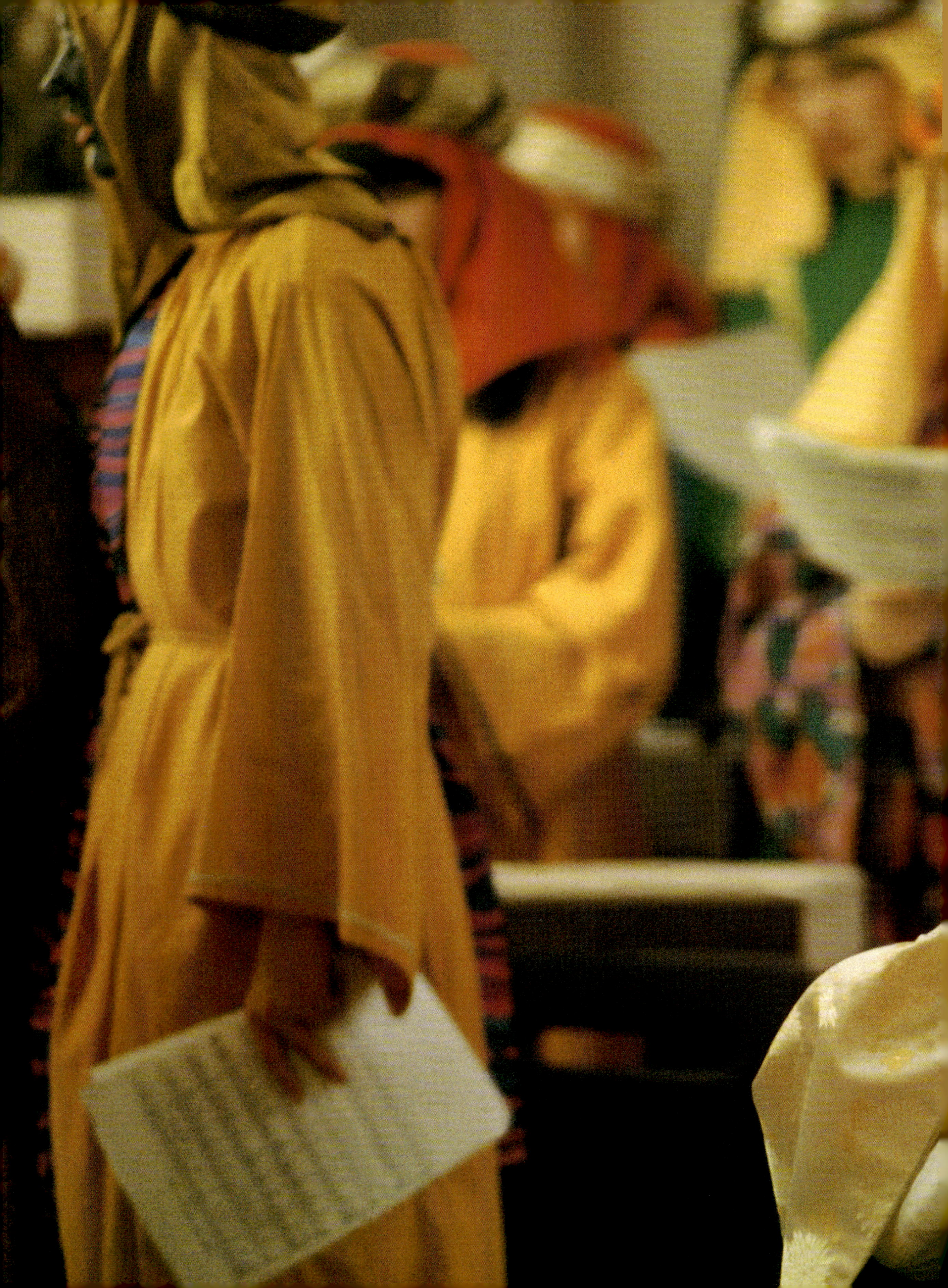

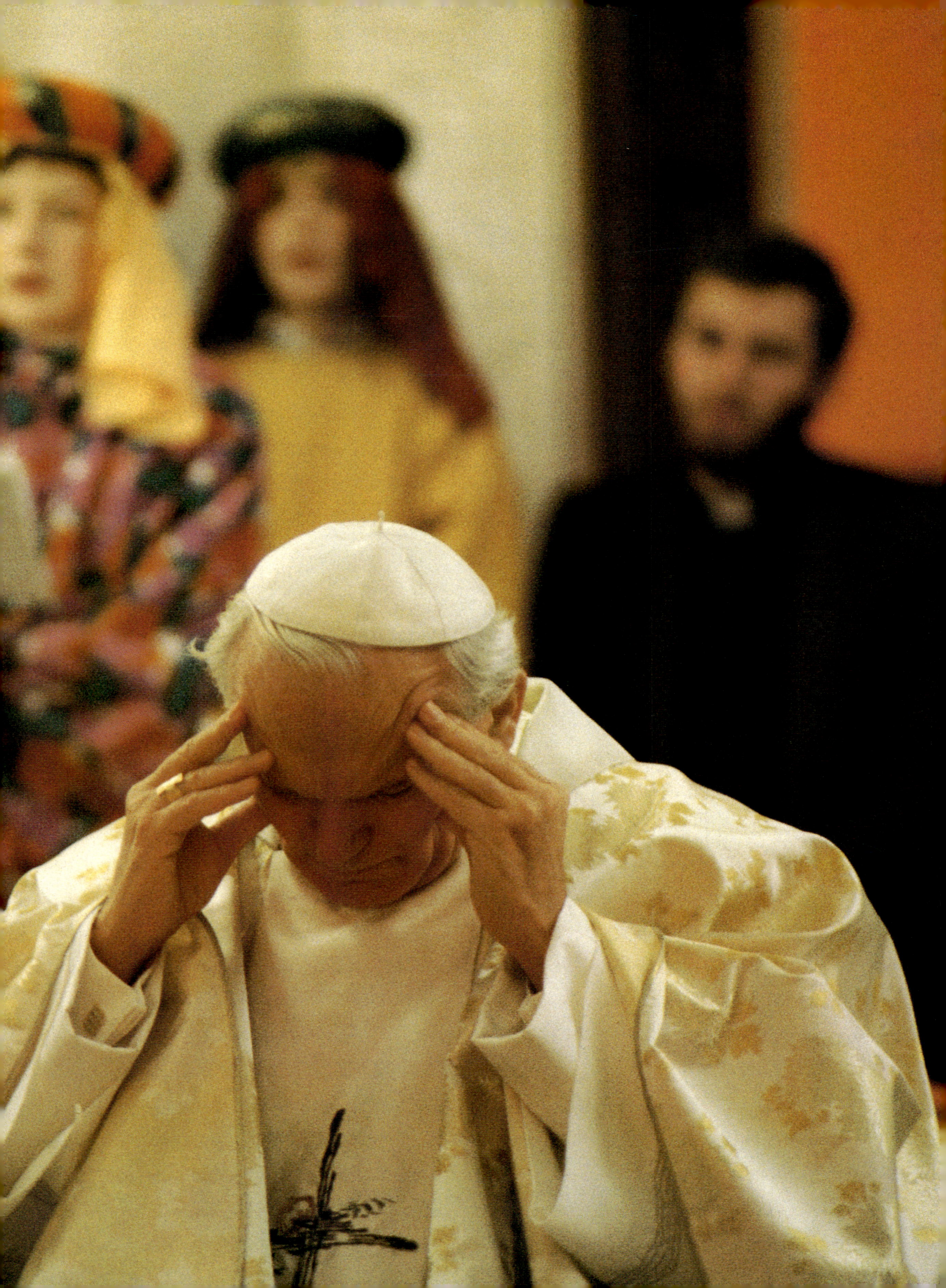

There was only one difference in seating: the Pope sat alone on one of the long sides of the table, with no one next to him. The menu was very simple: milk, coffee, cheese, jam.

The bread, which was already on the table, was the Roman "rosette" that Karol Wojtyla has loved since he was a young priest. "I came to Rome especially to eat these bread rolls with no center," he said to a fellow student who offered him a slice of wholemeal bread, "and you're offering me the ordinary stuff." Breakfast lasted no longer than half an hour. John Paul II worked until 11 a.m.: he used to read documents, examine dossiers and write – although less, of course, than he used to. As age and infirmity increased, his assistants had tried to reduce his workload, so private audiences and interviews with bishops visiting "*in limina*" were much briefer so as not to tax his failing strength. Similarly, the length of his official speeches and homilies was reduced.

The chapel stood in front of his private study, and he often visited it to concentrate his mind and to seek inspiration and help in making decisions. The Pope received many requests for prayers, which were first sifted through by his closest assistants. And then he found notes left on the confessional which gave a short explanation of the request for the prayer, "the intention," and the name of the person involved.

56 *When mass is over, John Paul II greets a group of Korean guests.*

56-57 *In the Library once more, the Pope has a few words with his guests.*

58-59 *Breakfast is a valuable time to start the day's work. The Pope talks with Cardinal Stephen Kim about the program for a visit to Korea. Seated on his right, his private secretary Stanislaw Dziwisz and, on his left, his secretary at the time, Emery Kabongo.*

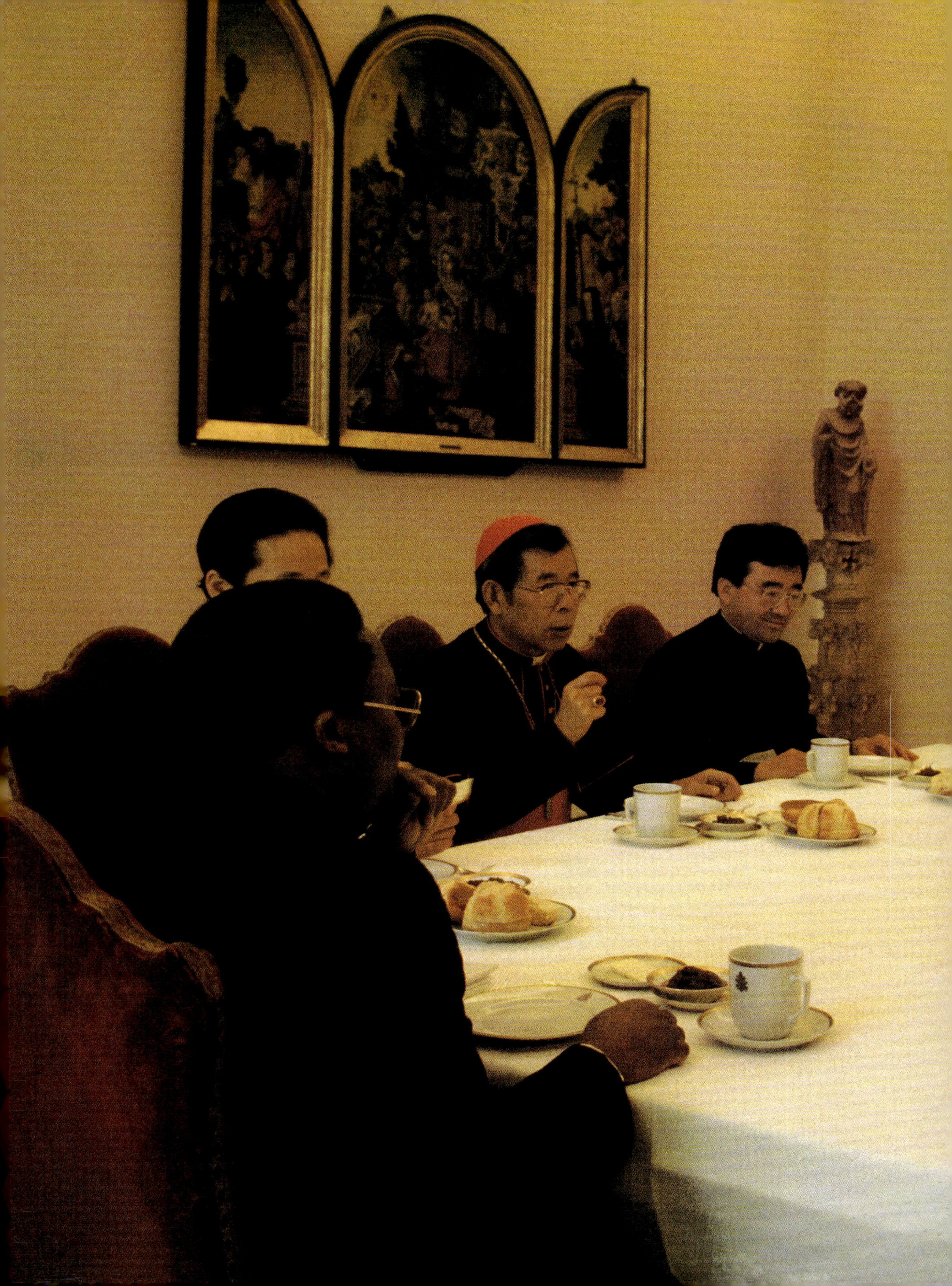

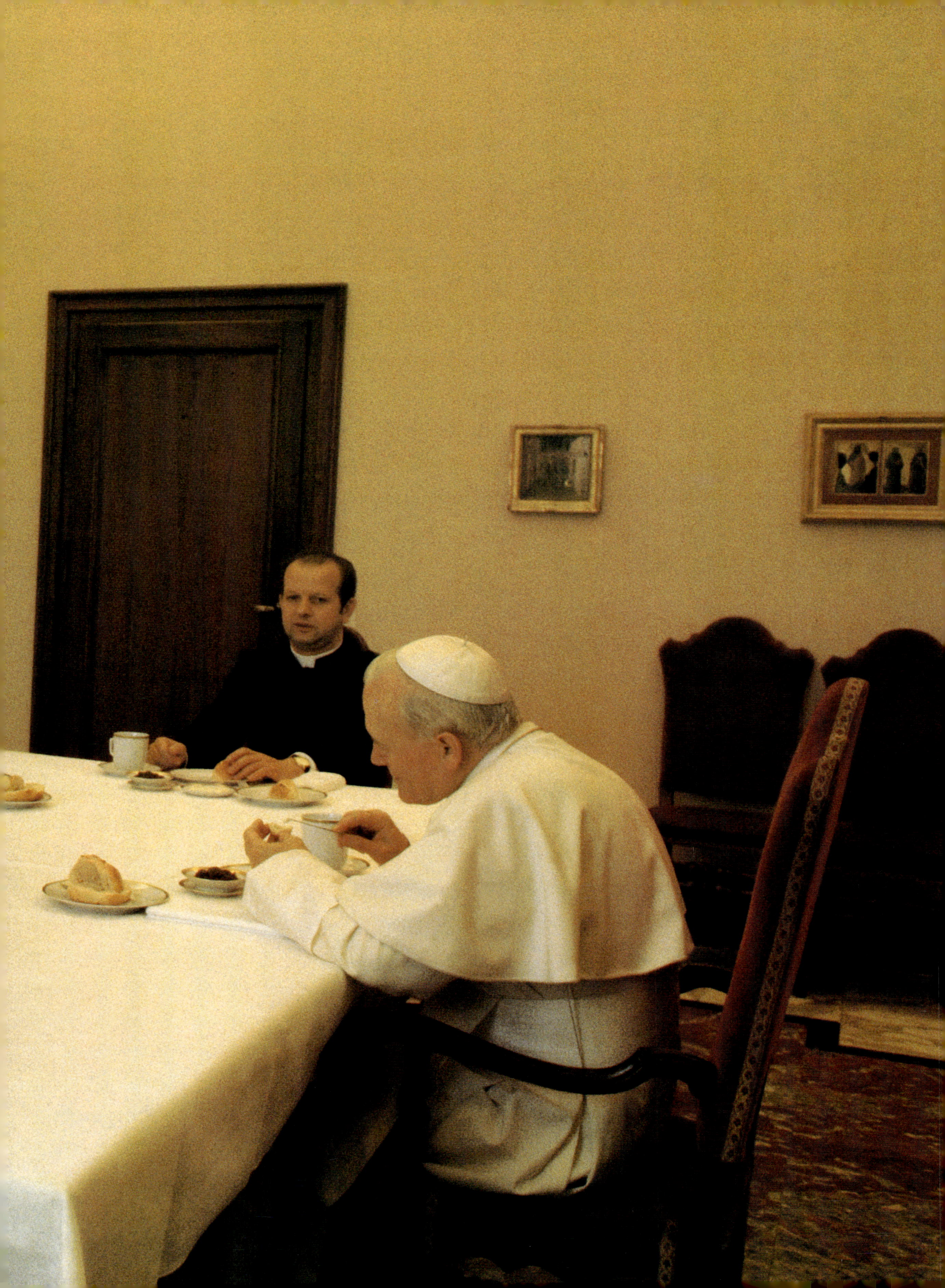

60-61 *The Pope goes back into the papal residence, accompanied by Monsignor Jacques Martin. The Raphael Loggia, so-called because it was decorated by the painter from Urbino, is on three floors and looks out over the San Damaso courtyard, opposite a wing of the Pope's private residence.*

Afterwards, the pontiff left "home" to begin the official part of his day. It is a modest house, all things considered: the papal apartments take up the top two floors of the east wing of the palace built by Sixtus V (1585-90). The dining room, bedroom, and study are comfortable but very sober. There is no longer the opulence of the red damask, which Paul VI had removed. Pastel colors predominate, with dark furniture of simple design. Some of the floors, which Paul VI preferred in wood, are now covered with pale tiles. It is easy to pick out the papal apartment from St. Peter's Square. The last window on the far corner of the palace, on the last floor, is the bedroom; the second window lights the private study (the one from which the Sunday Angelus is pronounced); and the next two central ones give onto the drawing room. The chapel is opposite the study, on the inside of the palace, while the dining room faces in the direction of the Tiber, toward Via della Conciliazione and the Passetto di Borgo. The overwhelming impression is one of great simplicity, a little disappointing, perhaps, for the admirers of the 17th-century Baroque of the Church of Rome. Paul VI swept away the last vestiges of the court, consigning to history the "noble ecclesiastical antechamber" and "His Holiness's majordomo," all the "ecclesiastical servants," the "secret valets," the "common chaplains" (one person alone looked after Pope John Paul II: Angelo Gugel, who has been in the Vatican a lifetime), as well as the three army corps (dissolved in 1970), including the Noble Guard of the Sword and Cape and the Palatine Guard. The pontifical household was run by two men: Monsignor James Harvey and Monsignor Dziwisz, the latter appointed as assistant Prefect. They were responsible for looking after many aspects of the Pope's public life, including the weekly Wednesday audiences in St. Peter's Square or in the Nervi Hall, which regularly attracted thousands of pilgrims and tourists. A typical year for the pontiff involved around five hundred audiences in addition to the general Wednesday ones. The term "audience" is a vague one, covering everything from a visit by a head of state to a meeting with representatives from one of the professions.

63 For the first time ever, and to the amazement of those pilgrims present, one Good Friday the Pope entered St. Peter's and began to hear confession like an ordinary priest. Since then the "Pope's confession" has been repeated every year as part of the Easter ceremonies.

As eleven o'clock drew near, the Pope left his second-floor apartment and went to the private Library, a large room used by the Popes who were "imprisoned" in the Vatican by the *bersaglieri* at Porta Pia during the Italian war of unification, and by their successors in this century. The main piece of furniture, and the most famous, is a desk in the monastic style, which has been silent witness to historic talks and surprising encounters. The Empress Zita, widow of the last Austrian monarch, Charles I, came to the Vatican and was welcomed by Karol Wojtyla with the words, "It is my pleasure to greet my father's sovereign," a reference to his father's service in Galicia, now part of Poland but once part of the Austro-Hungarian empire. The Library was the true throne room for this solitary monarch, solitary even in his secret pain. A foreign prelate tells the story of how in 1985 he would go every day to teach the Polish pontiff the rudiments of his language in preparation for one of the Pope's trips abroad, so that he could surprise the pilgrims who came to hear him. As the Pope stood up during the lesson he was unable to hide a grimace of severe pain. "Holiness, you are in pain," said the prelate. "Never repeat that," replied John Paul, his voice suddenly serious.

History, in the form of its great protagonists, has walked the Library's checkered tiles in nearly twenty seven years of this pontificate. A crowd of heads-of-state, ambassadors, bishops visiting *ad limina apostolorum* (after each five-year period in office, every bishop has to travel to Rome, back to the "threshold," the tomb of the apostles Saints Peter and Paul, to give an account of the situation in his diocese), nuncios, politicians, the heads of religious orders, and the Pope's "ministers." The Pope followed the news daily on television and in the newspapers, but the audiences, especially with the diocesan bishops, were his eyes and ears on the world – a direct contact which often did not end in the Library. "There are two things you never know with the Holy Father," once said one Monsignor jokingly. "What time he will eat and how many people he will invite to eat with him." John Paul's predecessors ate alone, or in very restricted company. John Paul II has transformed lunch into an instrument of government and of work. The last audience in his schedule would sometimes continue at the table, with guests from widely varying fields: specialists in a particular field if he was preparing an encyclical or other document, members of his own staff, nuncios, bishops, or just friends, such as Professor Styczen, Wojtyla's pupil in Lublin and his successor to the chair of moral theology, and Dr. Wanda Poltawska, a psychiatrist and expert in "natural" family planning methods and the Pope's consultant on women's affairs. Her friendship with John Paul II is an old one, and she probably has been the beneficiary of one of Padre Pio's miracles. In 1962 she was waiting to be operated on for cancer. Wojtyla, a bishop at the time, asked the friar who bore the stigmata to pray for her recovery, and the tumor disappeared mysteriously.

In the afternoon John Paul II rested a little, then took a walk, usually on the large terrace of the papal palaces, where he would read the breviary and meditate. Halfway through the afternoon he went back to work, met the closest members of his staff, wrote – or dictated, when his disease grew more serious – and drafted documents. At the moment of his death, he was gathering material to issue an encyclical on charity. After dinner, the rosary and the recital of the compieta ended the Pope's official day, but not his study. He was a fervent, omnivorous reader: St. Augustine, Martin Buber, Walt Whitman, St. Thomas Aquinas, Dostoevsky, Rilke, Mircea Eliade, Levinas, Wittgenstein, and Cyprian Norwid. He would read at any time, even during journeys. Monsignor Dziwisz always had room in his bag for whatever book the Pope was reading.

In time, physical movements were greatly reduced and eventually ceased completely. Consequently, the swimming pool in Castelgandolfo was used much less than before, but he was still able

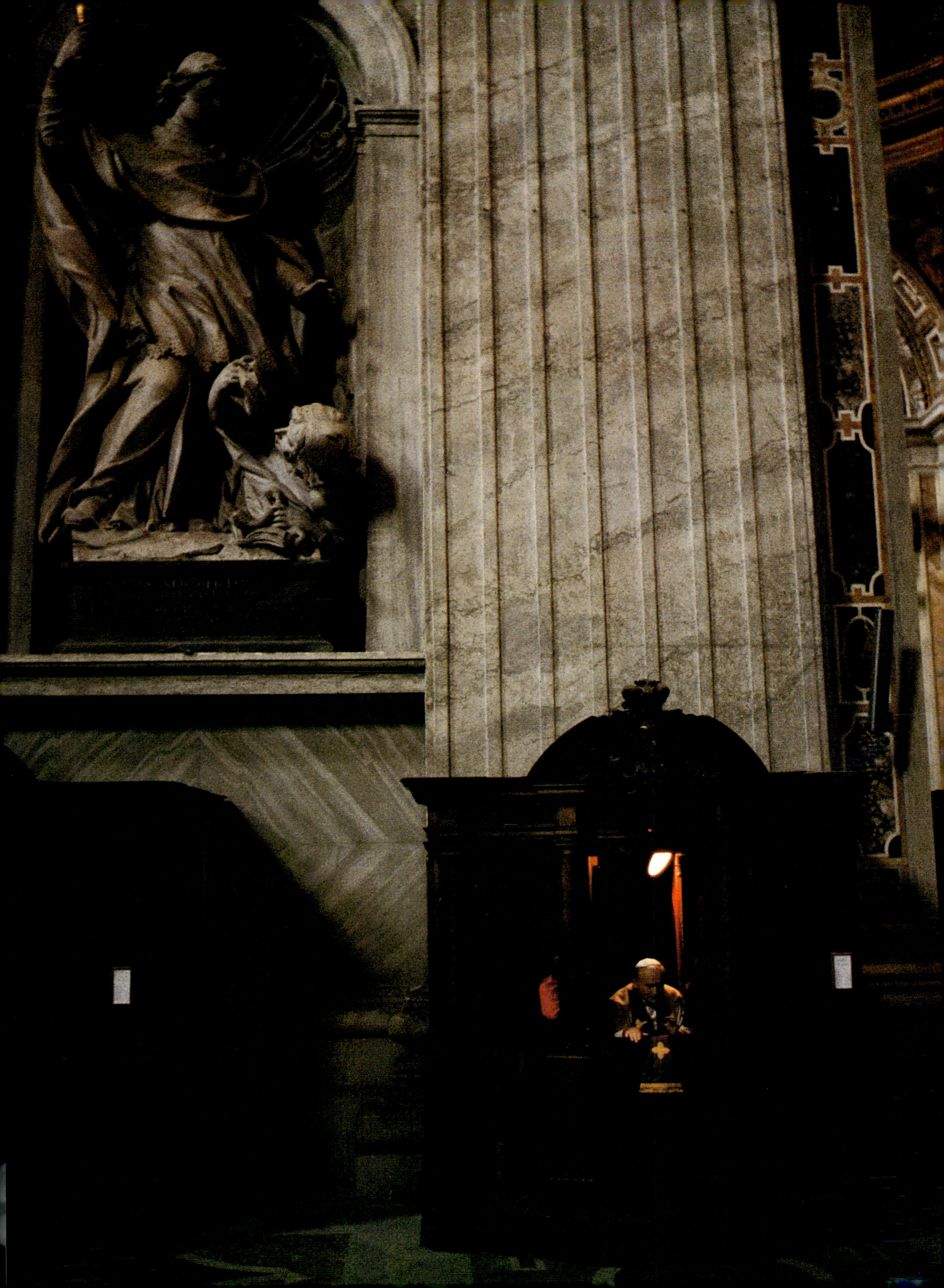

to enjoy himself and continued to see old friends. He had not yet given up winter trips to the mountains near Rome, despite his frailty. Though this never happened again after 2000, at the beginning of the 1990s a boy waiting in the lift line might recognize John Paul II standing next to him in a white ski suit. The Pope grew up in the mountains and needed to soak up the atmosphere every now and then, so each Tuesday, the least busy day of his week, he quietly slipped out of the Vatican in a short convoy of cars with dark windows on his way to find the snow, if there were any. Or at least to enjoy a little freedom with a view more expansive than that in the Via della Conciliazione.

In 1988 John Paul organized a dinner in the Vatican for twenty ex-pupils from the Wadowice high school, his final-year classmates. There had been forty-two of them; twenty were dead, ten having died during the Second World War. Jerzy Kluger, a Jewish friend of the Pope's who lives in Rome, led them through the Bronze Gate to a party where the main dish was pizza – the real, Neapolitan pizza – even though it had been made by the Polish nuns, who alternate Mediterranean dishes with typical central European ones. It was an emotional and nostalgic occasion, and so, they say, was Christmas, mainly Polish in style, except for the presence of the crib. The dinner was *maigre*, without meat. There was always carp, prepared in gelatine or with a sweet gray sauce containing sultanas, and there was always a cheesecake of which the Pope was particularly fond, along with poppy-seed cake. Pius X's biographers say that he would be seized by homesickness for Venice whenever he heard a train whistle, even in the distance. Pius XI would talk about his excursions in his beloved Lombardy mountains. Pius XII, John XXIII, Paul VI, and John Paul I were surrounded by brothers, sisters, nieces, and nephews, constituting a family (sometimes rather in the way). John Paul II had only a distant female cousin to whom he was not very close, and so at Christmas he broke the *Oplatek* – a rectangular host bearing scenes of the Holy Family – at a table with his secretaries, the five Polish nuns, and Angelo Gugel. Solitude is indeed the Pope's fate, but there were times when this Pope seemed more alone than the others.

64-65 *During a break from work, in the privacy of his bedroom, John Paul II allows his gaze to wander over the roofs of the capital.*

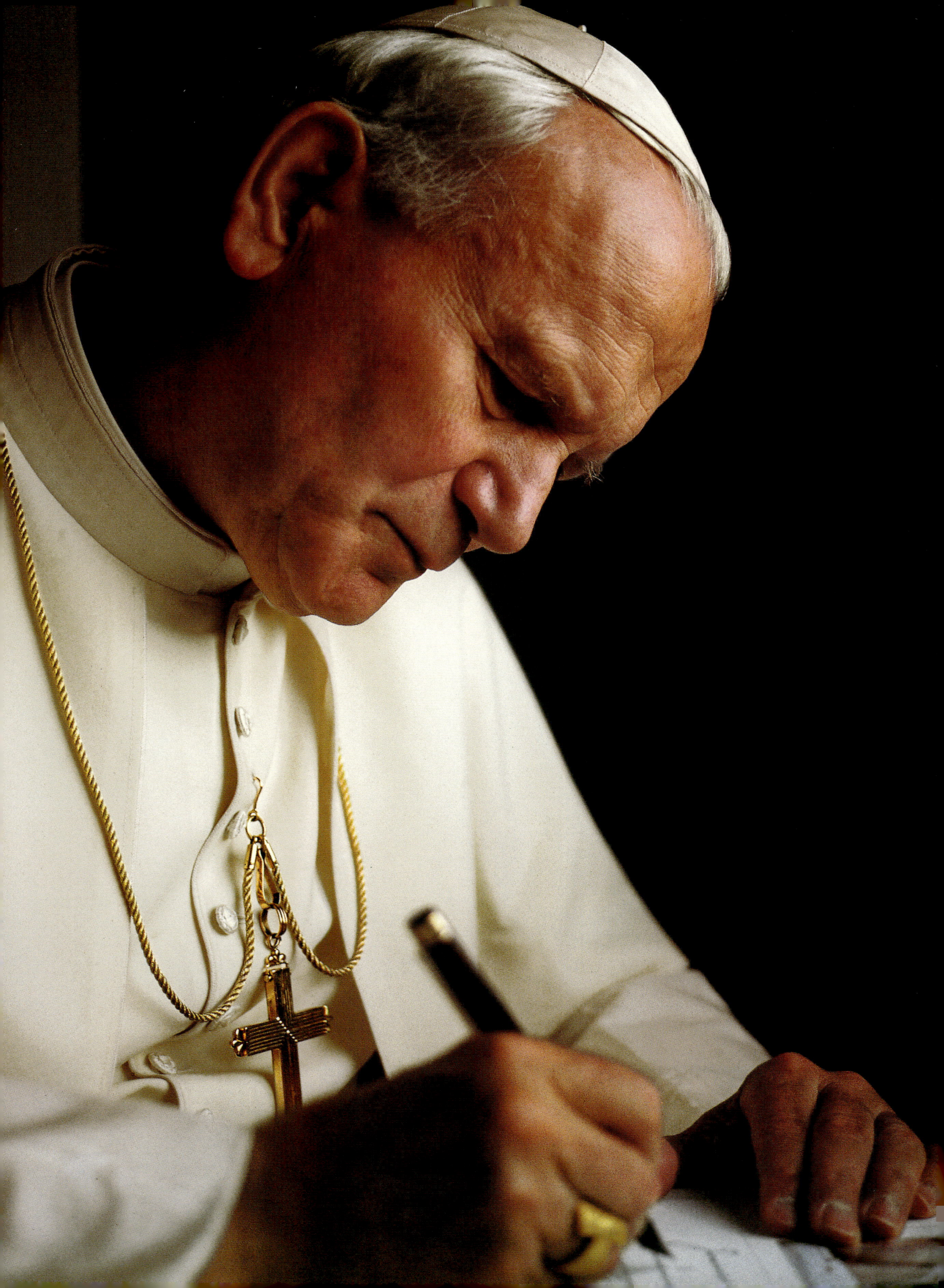

66 Deep in thought, the Pope puts his signature to a document. During his pontificate he has published twelve encyclicals, eight apostolic exhortations, and thirty apostolic letters. Each bears the Pope's arms on the cover — the triple crown, the keys, and his crest, consisting of a cross and the letter "M" for Maria, engraved on a shield — and the holograph signature of John Paul II in Latin.

67 John Paul II reads through some documents during a walk in the Vatican gardens. At the beginning of his pontificate the Pope liked to walk in the gardens, but he later abandoned the custom when it became inconvenient.

68-69 The Pope praying in the Hall of Investiture, where once the cardinal elected to the throne of Peter by the conclave received his new vestments.

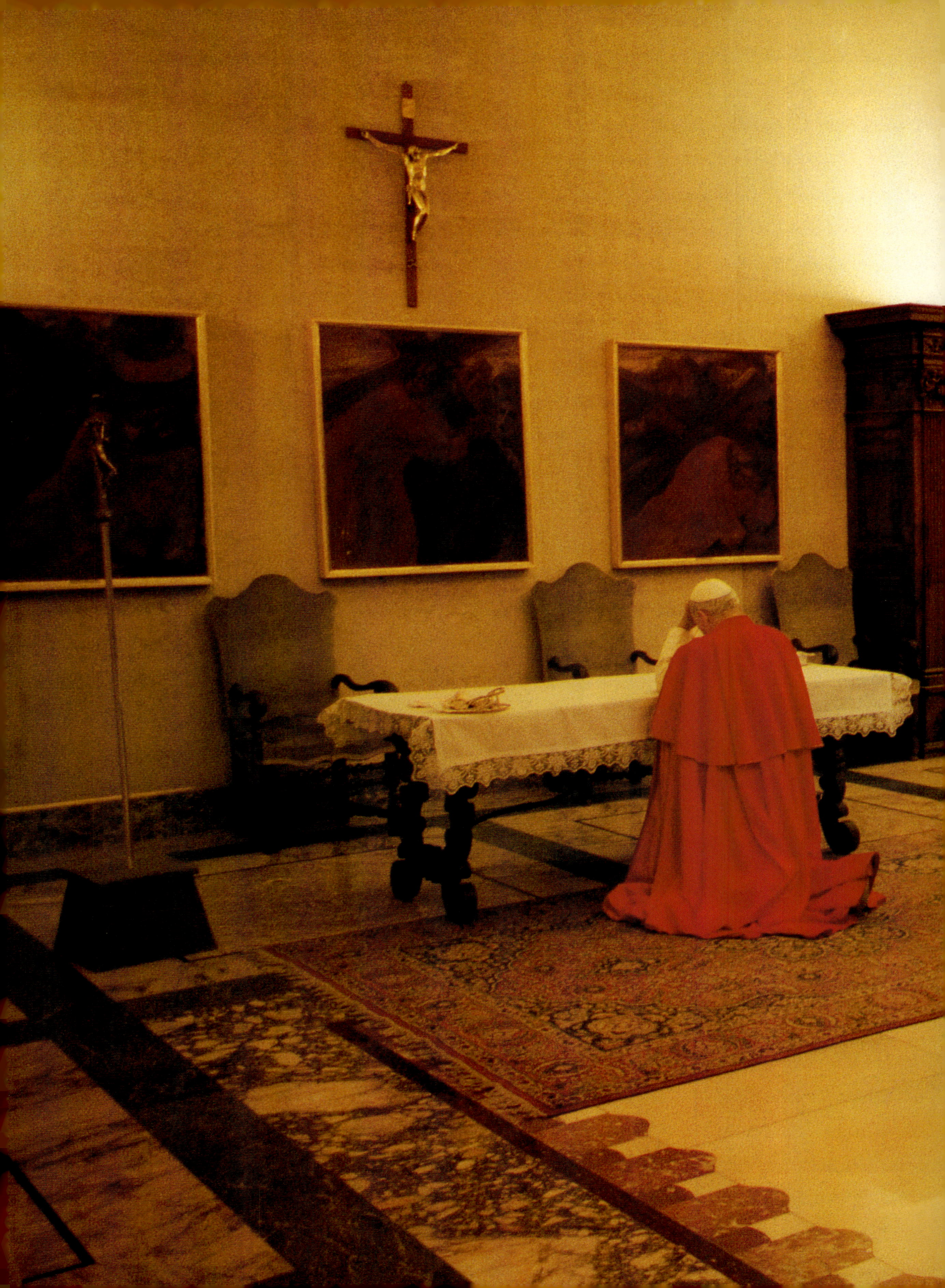

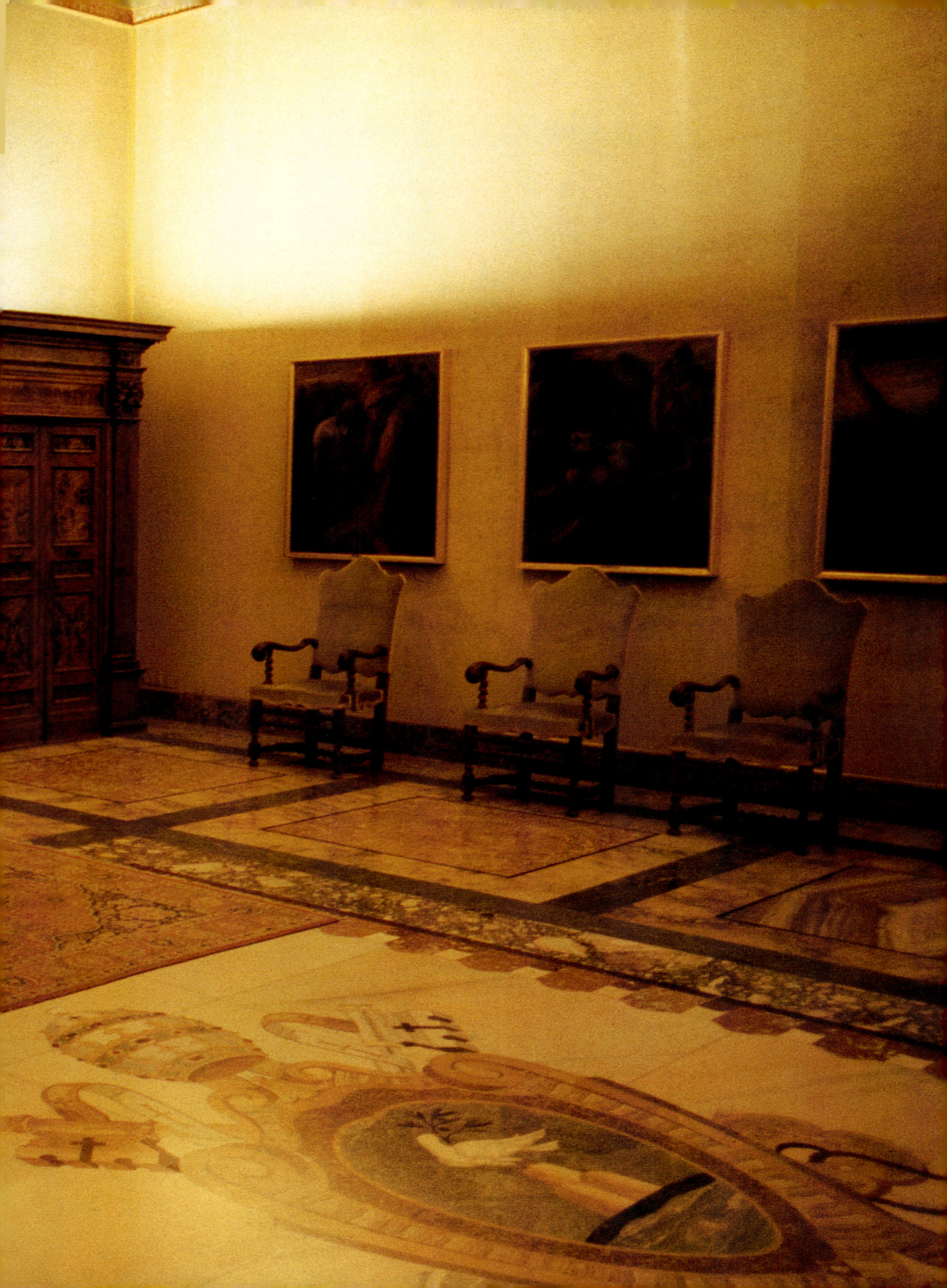

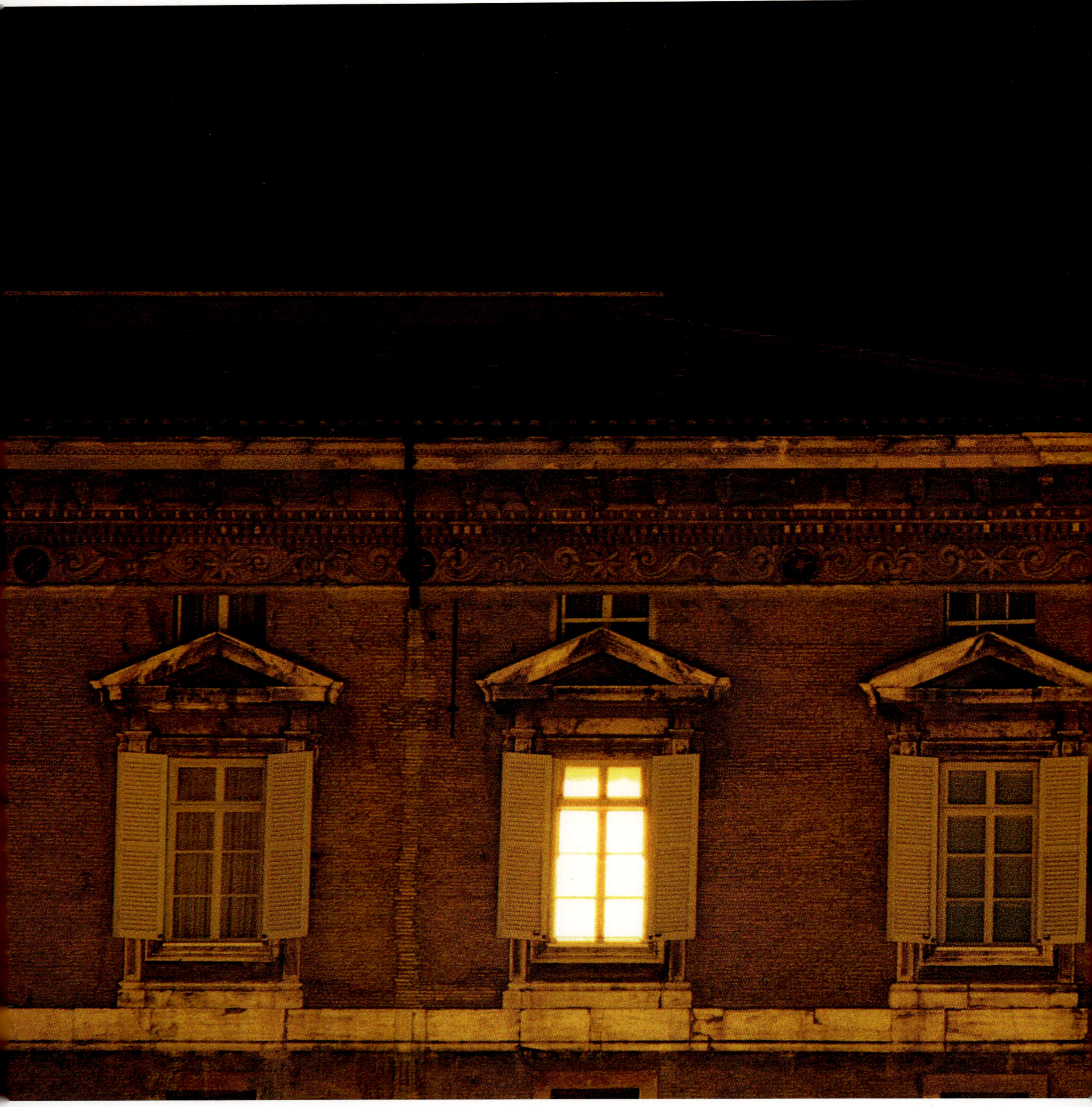

70-71 *A late stroller in St. Peter's Square will often see a light shining in the Pope's private study.*

71 *John Paul II ends his day with prayer in the private chapel before retiring. When he is in the Vatican, John Paul II spends a good deal of time thinking and praying in the chapel.*

72-73 Seoul, South Korea, 1984. "Your ancestors embraced such overwhelming spiritual realities, like Confucianism and Buddhism, that they truly made them their own, delving deep within them, living them."

74-75 A special area is prepared for the Pope on long flights. Here he is reading the Breviary during a journey to Argentina.

76-77 U.S.A., 1995. The Pope leaves the aircraft that has taken him from New York to Baltimore.

Papal Journeys

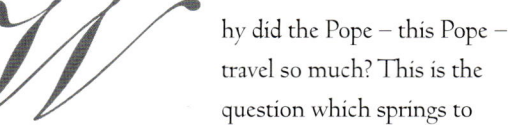

Why did the Pope – this Pope – travel so much? This is the question which springs to mind. Everyone, in fact, can see how different the past pontificate was, not so much from Paul VI's reign, but from the immobility of Popes in recent centuries. Pope John Paul II's reply was a very short one, but one which has infinite implications: "The problem of the Universal Church is to make it visible." The Universal Church: if it were not such an irreverent idea one could think of it as a multinational company *with* a soul and *for* the soul, the most widespread multinational on the planet, with branches in every country, and a great number of problems. Never in its history has the Roman Catholic Church been so big and had such internal diversity. Think, for example, of the diversity in culture, way of life, and sense of what is sacred between a parish in Frankfurt, Germany, and one in M'Bwanza, Congo. It is Rome itself, the faith and the doctrine, which acts as the adhesive force in this mosaic, and in people's eyes it is the Pope who supplies the visible sign of this unity. During a journey to Lima the security service had to restrain two girls who in their enthusiasm wanted to scratch the Pope to get a piece of his skin, as a holy souvenir.

It is a multinational whose branches – the local churches – are constantly increasing, becoming more powerful and more protective of their own autonomy. It is in close competition with many other bodies, *ad maiorem Dei gloriam*, to provide salvation: Islam, wealthy and expanding in Africa; sects and new religious movements in South America; the traditional culture of Eastern Asia, a wall from which the Church, after centuries of effort, has managed to win only a few chips of conversion; and not forgetting what the Pope himself considers to be the most insidious rival of all: the materialism, the permissivism that reduces everything, including men and women, to consumer items.

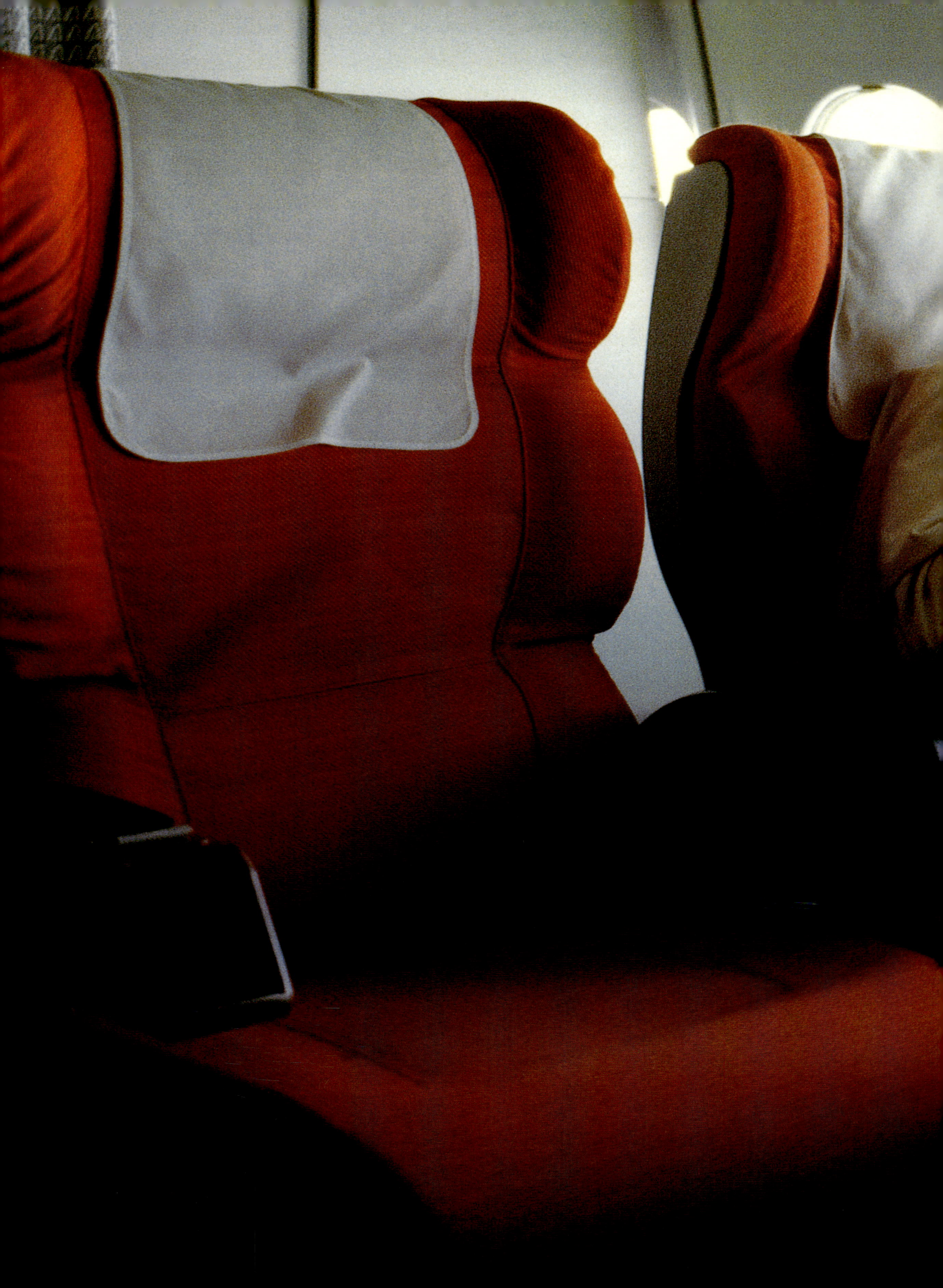

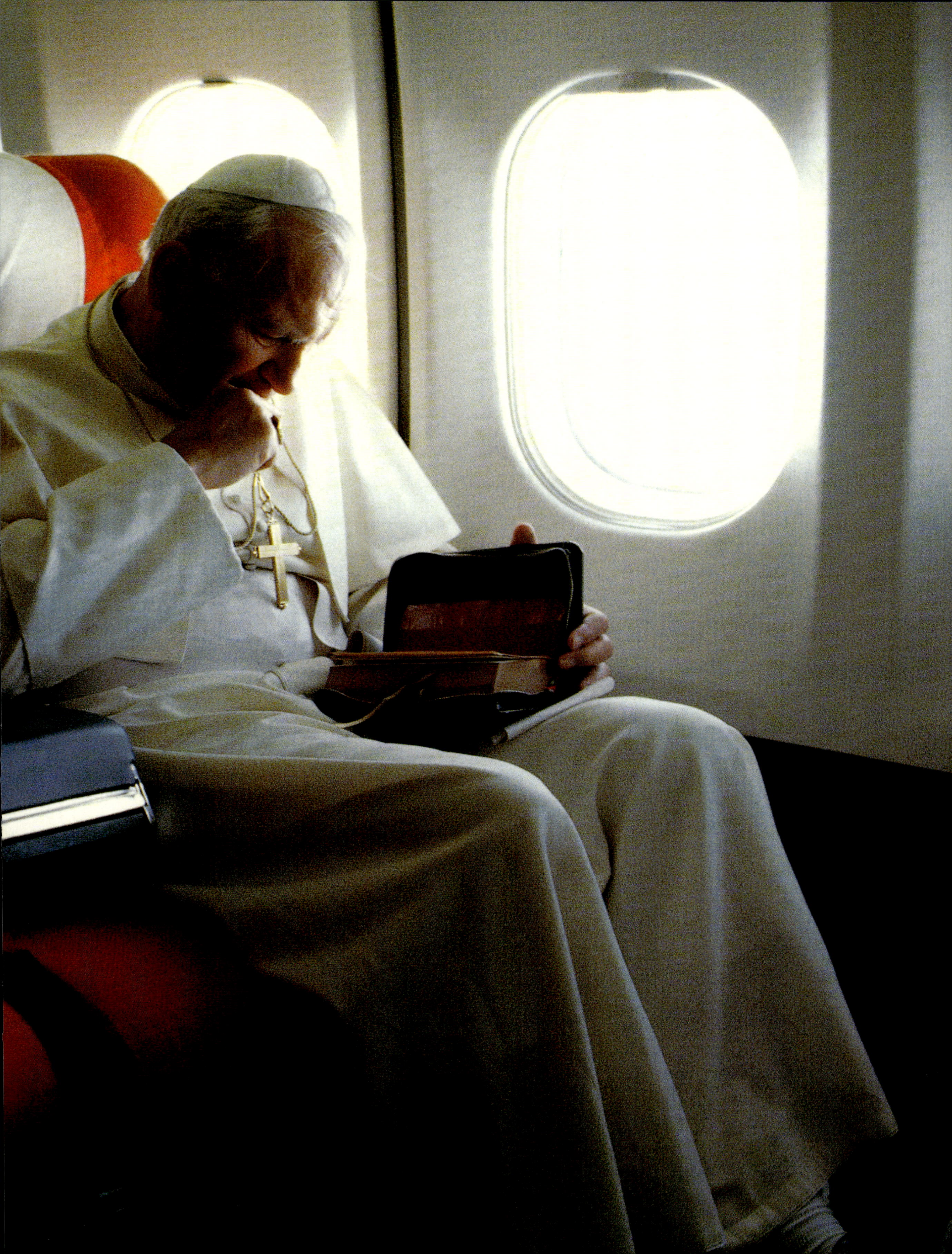

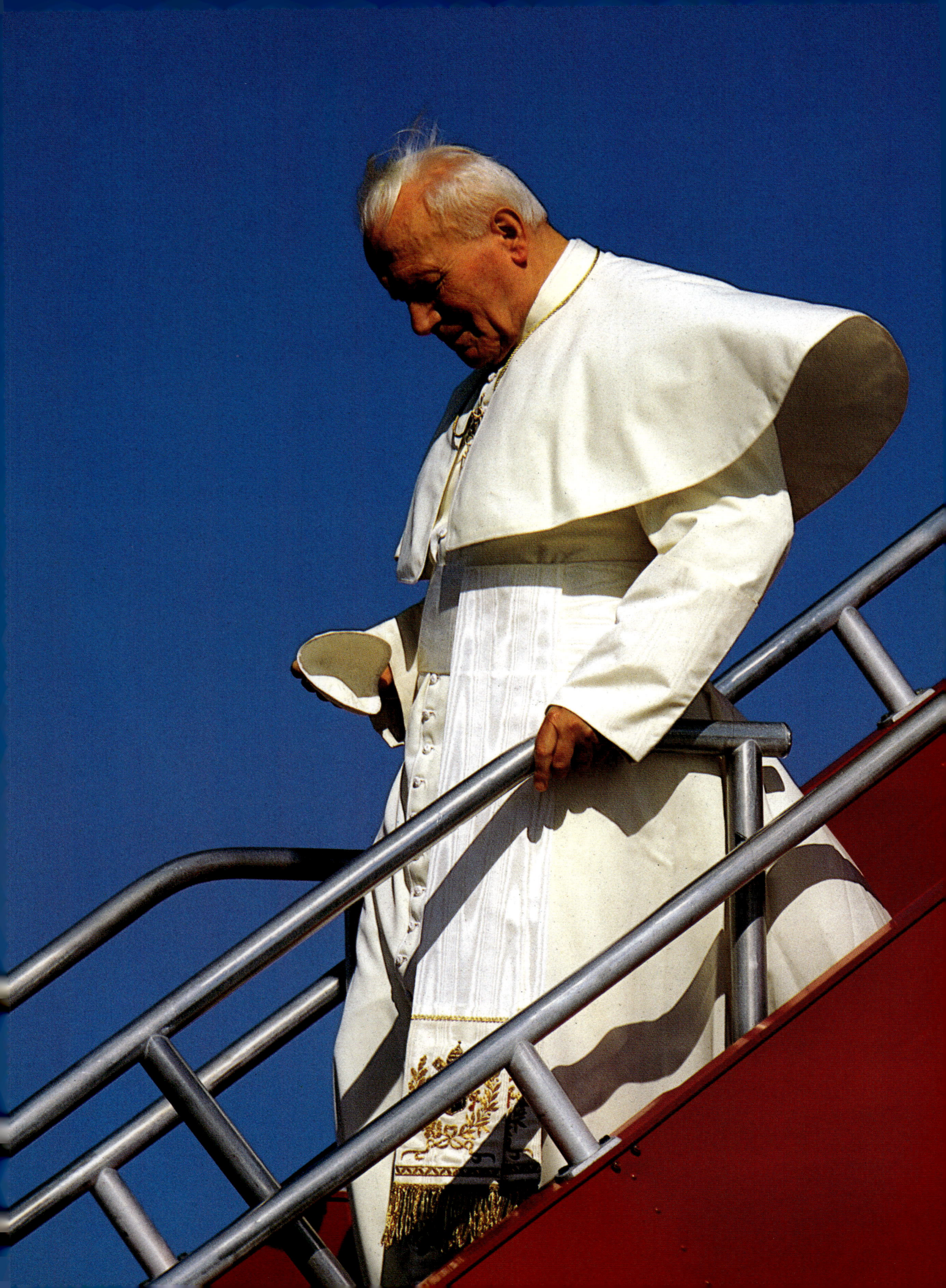

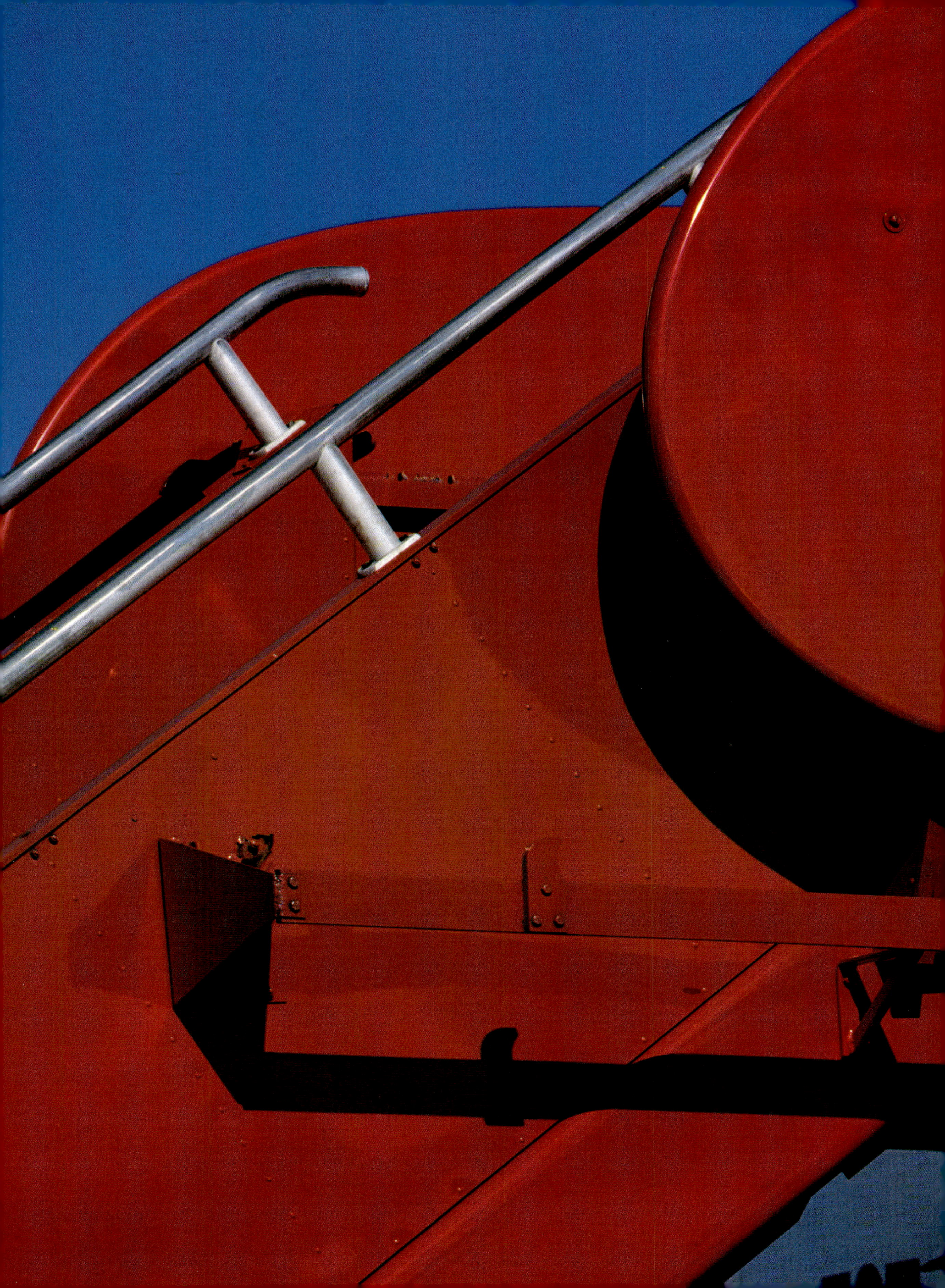

So the Pope would travel, in order to present Rome to every corner of the world, in every church, no matter how out of the way or how insignificant.

This is the message: Rome is, it exists and it is still, as in the times of Peter, for the Roman Catholic faith at least, *caput mundi*. Everywhere the Pope went, he put on the scales something that no other religion can offer: God's Vicar on Earth, a figure of tremendously powerful sacred charisma that inspires awe in the masses. Until his last journey, in 2005, when he went to Loreto, despite the fact that age and infirmity had to some extent dulled his edge as an orator, he could still move tens, even hundreds of thousands of the faithful – and it is difficult for anyone who has not witnessed it to understand – to paroxysms of enthusiasm with a single word, a gesture, or a sentence.

"One must travel to live and live to travel," John Paul II is reported to have confided to a friend once. When questioned about the truth of this anecdote by his biographer, André Frossard, he replied, "I don't remember, but I can't deny it, either."

The apostles traveled too, is the comment from the Vatican, and the Pope did not hesitate to defend this characteristic of his pontificate. "I know too that there are some people who do not approve of these journeys," he said, on his return from Latin America in 1985, "and this fact is what confirms my belief that they must be made." Whatever the cost.

To anyone who asked him, at the end of an exhausting two-week tour in 1986 – taking in Bangladesh, Singapore, Fiji, New Zealand, Australia, and the Seychelles – if the results were worth so much effort and such a high cost (paid by the local churches), he replied, "Yes, yes, it's worth it, it's worth it; I believe that we cannot count the cost when we are bought at an inestimable price.

Do you understand? There is no cost for this. It is stupid to talk about cost and to try and stop the Pope.

78-79 La Paz, Bolivia, 1988. "Drug consumption has become the trading of freedom, it has become the worst kind of slavery, of corruption, of death. The drug trade is, from every point of view, an abomination."

80-81 Guadalcanal, Solomon Islands, 1984. John Paul II was welcomed by Prime Minister Mamaloni and took the salute from a very British-style honor guard.

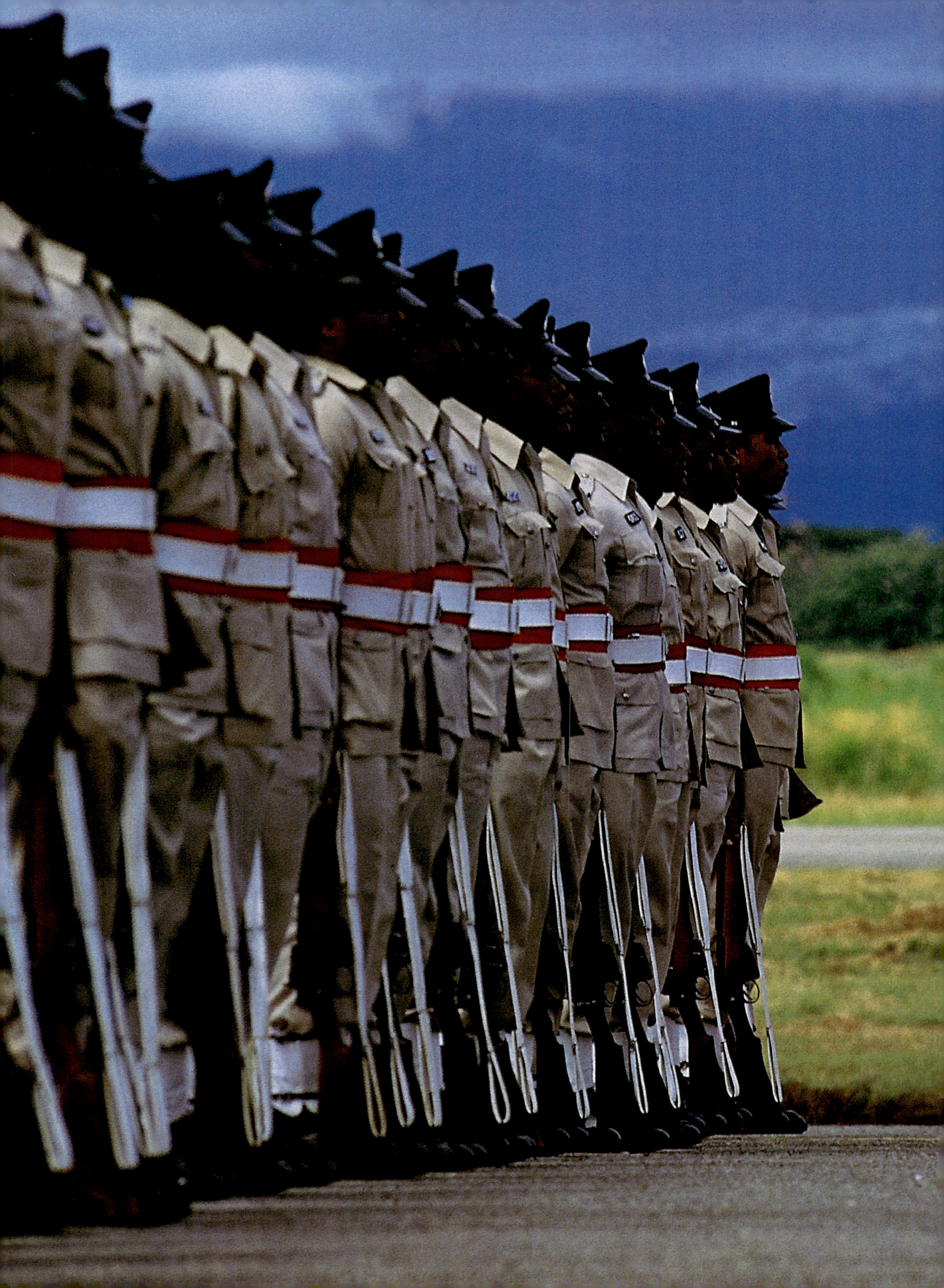

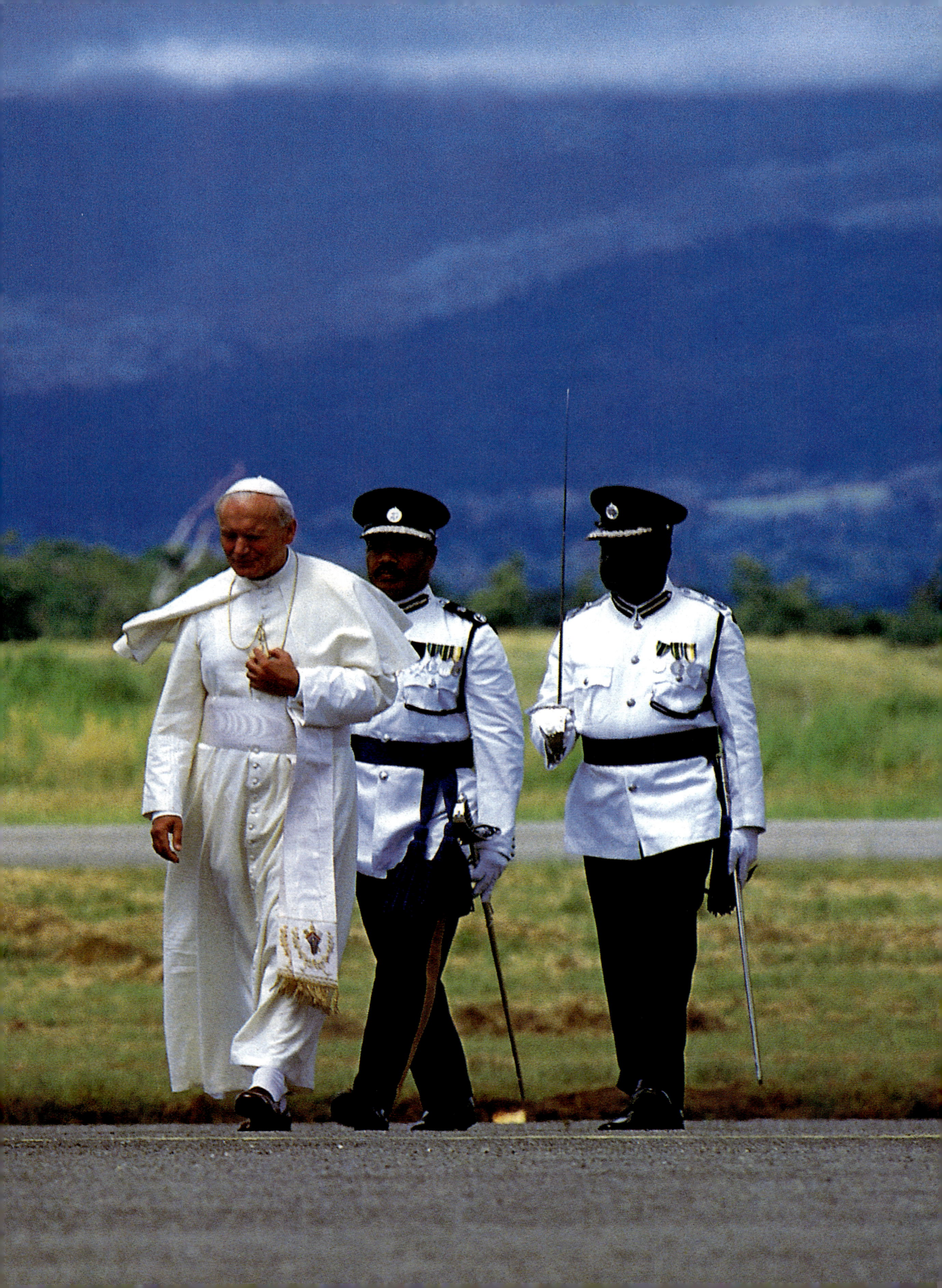

82-83 *"La Serena," Chile, April 1987. John Paul II intended this journey to be one of hope for national reconciliation in a country torn by political strife.*

The cost. He costs more than the Queen! Thank God, because the message he brings has a transcendent value; he brings things which are of great worth and importance."

The queen in question was Elizabeth II of Great Britain. Her visit to Australia shortly before the Pope's had cost much less.

John Paul II visited the Chilean dictator, Augusto Pinochet, in the Casa Rosada and the Sandinista regime in Managua, where he faced a violent demonstration during mass.

He shook hands with General Jaruszelski in June 1983, six months after the anti-Solidarity coup, and he met Alfred Stroessner, the pro-Nazi ruler of Paraguay. The list of dictators and presidents of pseudo-democratic Third-World regimes greeted on the tarmacs of innumerable airports is a long one.

The Pope has visited Angola and Mozambique, countries torn apart by civil wars, when the ceasefire was fragile and the guns still warm. He experienced the apagon – total electrical blackout – in Lima, caused by the Sendero Luminoso, and widespread hostile demonstrations in Holland, Switzerland, Austria, Federal Germany, and the United States, not to mention the storm over Maseru in Lesotho, which led to a damaged plane and a forced landing in Johannesburg when the apartheid regime was still in power – the reason for discounting a possible visit in the first place. "I cannot avoid risks. I have to meet the people, the rulers and the politicians," the Pope has explained. "Perhaps sometimes politics is a sinful thing, and perhaps there are sometimes sinful rulers. But one cannot ignore this political dimension of life, especially in the life of a nation.

When I went to Africa for the first time, I was delighted to see states which had been under colonial powers until a few years earlier finally enjoying their own sovereignty.

Perhaps it was an imperfect sovereignty, not yet translated into democratic principles, but at least those people were the bosses in their own homes."

"You can cut off my hands if Wojtyla manages to stay more than two consecutive weeks in the Vatican," was the spontaneous comment of his friend Jerzy Turowicz, on Wojtyla's election, and the prophecy has proved true. A reverse Copernican revolution, begun by Paul VI, has become a characteristic feature of the pontificate. Rome no longer waits, passively, for the local churches to come to her, she moves out toward the edges. Four international journeys and eight in Italy every year had become the norm, at last until his strength allowed him to travel. "El trotamundo de la paz" is what one South American newspaper called him (other equally vivid headlines read: "el Maradona de la fe" and "el goleador de la Iglesia"). He has covered twice and half the distance to the moon and back.

The Pope's journeys, with his staff and a small number of accompanying journalists, had become a separate category of events, with its own rules and protocol. Some were written, others were not, but this did not make them any less binding. John Paul II's first flight from Rome was in January 1979, just three months after his election, his destination the Dominican Republic, Mexico, and the Bahamas. Alitalia prepared a bed for him, as it does on all intercontinental flights, a real bed in the front of the cabin, using Paul VI's sheets. Despite his age and his troublesome health, Paul VI had been no mean traveler; the sheets were silk, and John Paul II let it be known that he preferred cotton ones. "He wants a humbler style," said his entourage, but the Holy Father dismissed the suggestion, saying simply that silk sheets stuck to his body.

The Pope always left Rome with Alitalia and usually returned by the national airline of the last country on his tour. He was accompanied by a considerable number of his "top-level management": the Secretary of State and the Under-Secretary of State, as well as the Prefect of the Papal Household and the indispensable presence of the Papal Master of Ceremonies, Monsignor Marini, who assisted him at all religious functions. Then there is the head of the Vatican Radio and of the *Osservatore Romano*, the

84-85 *Calcutta, India, 1986. During his visit, the Pope went to the house which the priests of the goddess Kali gave Mother Teresa to look after the dying homeless: "Oh most tender and compassionate God, bless all those who are dying, all those who are soon to meet Thee face to face."*

Pope's doctor, Professor Renato Buzzonetti; his private secretary, Monsignor Dziwisz; his valet, Angelo Gugel; and Father Tucci, who, since 1982, when he replaced Monsignor Marcinkus, had been in charge of organizing the papal trips. The entourage was, of course, accompanied by members of the Vatican security service and the Swiss Guard, who changed out of their multicolored costumes into sober suits for the occasion. Lastly, there were the variables: prelates of the congregations closely involved in the ceremonies lined up for that particular trip, cardinals, and members of the episcopal conferences of the countries to be visited.

For John Paul II the hours in the air were almost a holiday, the last restful period before the furious onslaught of meetings, speeches, and traveling that is the daily bread of every pastoral visit. Since the incident in April 1994, the organizers started wielding the axe vigorously, paring down the papal appointment book, but the days the Globetrotter Pope spent in his travels were packed with engagements and hard work. The front of the Alitalia cabin was converted into a small sitting room with a table crowned by a splendid flower arrangement in white and yellow, the papal colors, or, on occasion, the red and white of the Polish flag. A crucifix was hung on the wall opposite the Pope's chair, together with an icon of the Madonna of Fatima, an object of his particular devotion: on May 13, 1982, he laid the blood-

86 Morocco, 1985. An historic kiss: John Paul II is welcomed at Casablanca airport by the "Head of the Believers," King Hassan II of Morocco, who invited him to address young Muslims in the city stadium.

86-87 Casablanca, Morocco, 1985. The only mass meeting between the Pope and followers of Islam: "Christians and Muslims must bear witness to Him, in word and deed, in a world which is increasingly secularized and sometimes even atheist."

stained sash he was wearing on the day of the assassination attempt at the feet of the original statue. (Also the bullet fired at John Paul II on 13 May 1981 has been inserted in the crown of this statue).

Pope John Paul II would read, pray, recite the rosary and – on the outward leg of long journeys, used to talk to the press. Yes, the press. Fifty – and the number hardly ever varies – photographers and journalists from the printed press, television, and radio were allowed on the papal flight. Only those who were permanently accredited by the Vatican could even hope to be included on the list. This was the only occasion that journalists could have direct, face-to-face access with the Pope, after which down came the curtain of privacy, which in the last years has been an hermetic one. About half an hour after take-off, John Paul appeared on the cabin threshold which marks the border between the area reserved for the press and the "forbidden" zone where the entourage is lodged, and would answer three or four questions. Familiarity tends to banish awe, and nowadays no one is surprised if the Vicar of God on Earth talks to the press. It was not always so. When Paul VI made an appearance on one of his first trips, the press corps was shaken by a storm of emotion. Many fell to their knees and some were so overcome that they were unable to utter a word. In those days there was an unwritten rule that the Pope could not be questioned directly; he alone could speak. Paul VI

88-89 *Casablanca, Morocco, 1985. The sovereign of Morocco invited his illustrious guest to his palace for a private conversation before accompanying him to a meeting with participants in the Pan-Arab games.*

90-91 *Sion, Switzerland, 1984. A difficult trip: women, theologians, and priests all reproached the Pope for the Church of Rome's closed attitude.*

would walk through the rows of seats, stopping to say a few words and hand out the commemorative medals of the trip, and move on.

Even when traveling, the Pope would eat and sleep in his own "home": he has never accepted the hospitality of the host government. He usually lodged in the residence of the papal nuncio, sometimes in the bishop's palace or with a religious order. The same philosophy dictated that he never took part in official luncheons or dinners. Every one of the trips he has made until now has had its own unique physiognomy, but, obviously, some were more significant than others. The key to interpreting the enigma of this Pope is to be found in his journeys rather than his Vatican-based activity. They bring him face to face with real political, social, and human situations without the mediation and shield provided by his Roman court, and at the same time they provide an open window onto his own thoughts and feelings. "I . . . could . . . not . . . not go" was his comment on his first trip to Poland in 1979. Since then he has returned to his homeland once every four years, and each visit brings with it intense emotions. In May 1997, for instance, he was unable to hide his feelings upon arriving at Bielsko Biala, the small town where his brother died when he himself was still a boy. There have been terrible disappointments too. The Pope's three Polish journeys trace the parabola of his pontificate. In 1979, only a few months after he had been elected to the Throne of Peter, John Paul II crossed Warsaw in a military vehicle painted white for the occasion. It was a triumph. The streets were carpeted with flowers and more flowers rained down from the windows lining the route. When the Pope entered the cathedral next to Wyszynski, the elderly cardinal was deeply affected, and tears could be seen, or rather intuited, on the Pope's face as he wiped his cheek with the back of his hand. The message he took with him was this: "It is impossible to understand this nation, with its splendid and at the same time terribly difficult history, without Christ."

Four years later the scenario had changed. The Solidarity trade union had been outlawed, and the country was under martial law, controlled by the police and the army. It was a penitential journey; even the weather was grey. Huge crowds gathered in a climate of irrtional, almost millenarian, expectancy, as if the Pope could turn the situation on its head by magic. There were a million – at least – Czestochowa, two million at Kraków, where he beatified two 19th-century heroes of the movement against the Tsar. "For Kalinowski and Chmielowski," he said, "insurrection was a stage in their journey toward sainthood. They were driven by a heroic love for their homeland. The sacrifice of their own lives for that of their friends manifested itself in their participation in the insurrection." The Church acted as an umbrella for the Poles during the years of Jaruszelski's rule.

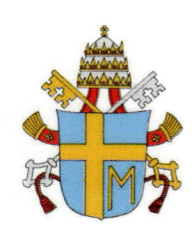

In 1991 the Pope went back to a homeland that had been liberated from the Marxist regime. The year 1989 had come and gone: the Wall had come down, and what Reagan had dubbed the "Evil Empire" had collapsed. But this 20th-century Moses, after leading his people to victory, found them gathered around the Golden Calf of abundance and of permissiveness. "We must conquer the works of the flesh, and they are not only fornication, impurity, and libertinage, but enmity, discord, divisions, envy, and drunkenness." Every day he cast

92-93 *Austria, 1983. The Pope remembers the victory of John III of Poland against the Turks, at Vienna. "That victory of Polish troops saved Europe's civilization and Christianity."*

94-95 *Thailand, May 1984. John Paul visits the refugee camp at Phanat Nikhom.*

95 *Thailand, May 1984. John Paul II visits the 86-year-old monk Vasana Tara, the country's supreme Buddhist patriarch, at his residence.*

aside the official speeches and cried his indignation aloud, improvising *ex abundantia coris* – because his heart was overflowing: "Good behavior is required! Freedom needs maturity. Liberty cannot only be a pretense; that would put mankind into chains – and we must not confuse immorality with freedom. I say this because this land is my mother, this land is the mother of my brothers and of my sisters, and you must all understand that your approach to these things is irresponsible and that these things hurt me and they should hurt you too."

Poland had changed. In 1983 an entire park was not enough when the Pope celebrated mass, but by 1991 the main square in the Old Town was more than sufficient. According to one of the Pope's closest advisers, who wishes to remain anonymous, in order to understand Wojtyla, that journey and that brutal realization must be taken into account; it seems after all that the battle against Communism was a relatively simple one. Today's adversary is more insidious and more powerful. Freed from the fear of favoring the pro-Marxist wings of the Church, John Paul II can launch his most difficult crusade: the challenge of the final years of the millennium against the "virus of rampant materialism, of indifference to ethical values and the consumer society," as he admonished in his lightning trip to Prague in April 1990, celebrating "his" victory amid the still-smoking ruins of one of the most anti-clerical governments in the Warsaw Pact. The elderly Pope has taken up his crosier and launched a new crusade to bring Christianity back to the Western Europeans. It seemed impossible that such a long pontificate could still harbor any surprises and yet, in the twentieth year of his reign, one of the great "walls" fell and Pope Wojtyla disembarked on the "Pearl of the Caribbean," the only large island in the New World he had not yet visited. It was a trip filled with compassion – John Paul II said all that he wanted to say, and Fidel Castro behaved like an impeccable and considerate host.

After Cuba, the Pope embarked on a flurry of trips, perhaps the most important of his pontificate. Some he was forced to cancel, such as the visit to Armenia planned for July 1999 but put off following the death of Patriarch Karekin. John Paul wished very much to visit the Armenians, who were the first people to suffer genocide in the 20th century, at the hands of the Turks, who still deny their involvement. Armenia was the first Christian state in the world (eleven years before Emperor Constantine promulgated his edict) and the Armenian Church is ancient and plays an important ecumenical role. Armenia was also the first republic to declare itself independent from the former USSR, so a trip to the country would have been fraught with significance. John Paul II, however, had to wait until the end of the century before visiting Armenia. Instead the Pope went to Romania and Georgia, both countries with an Orthodox majority, where he showed strong signs of friendship and support for the "eastern lobe" of the Church even as the war in Kosovo raged not far away. Above all, he was able to make his dream come true and pay a jubilee visit to the homeland of Christianity. The stop at Mt. Sinai was very emotional while the visit to the Holy Land was equally intense and rewarding, even though his presence caused heated debate among both Jews and Moslem fundamentalists.

96-97 *Honduras, March 1983. The papal procession, headed by the "Popemobile," takes a wrong turn and ends up driving through the dusty streets of a small village.*

PAPUA NEW GUINEA

98 *John Paul II has visited Papua New Guinea twice, in 1984 and 1994. At Port Moresby he was presented with the typical flowered garland of welcome.*

98-99 *Mount Hagen, Papua New Guinea, 1994. John Paul II was welcomed by a group of dancers wearing the traditional costume.*

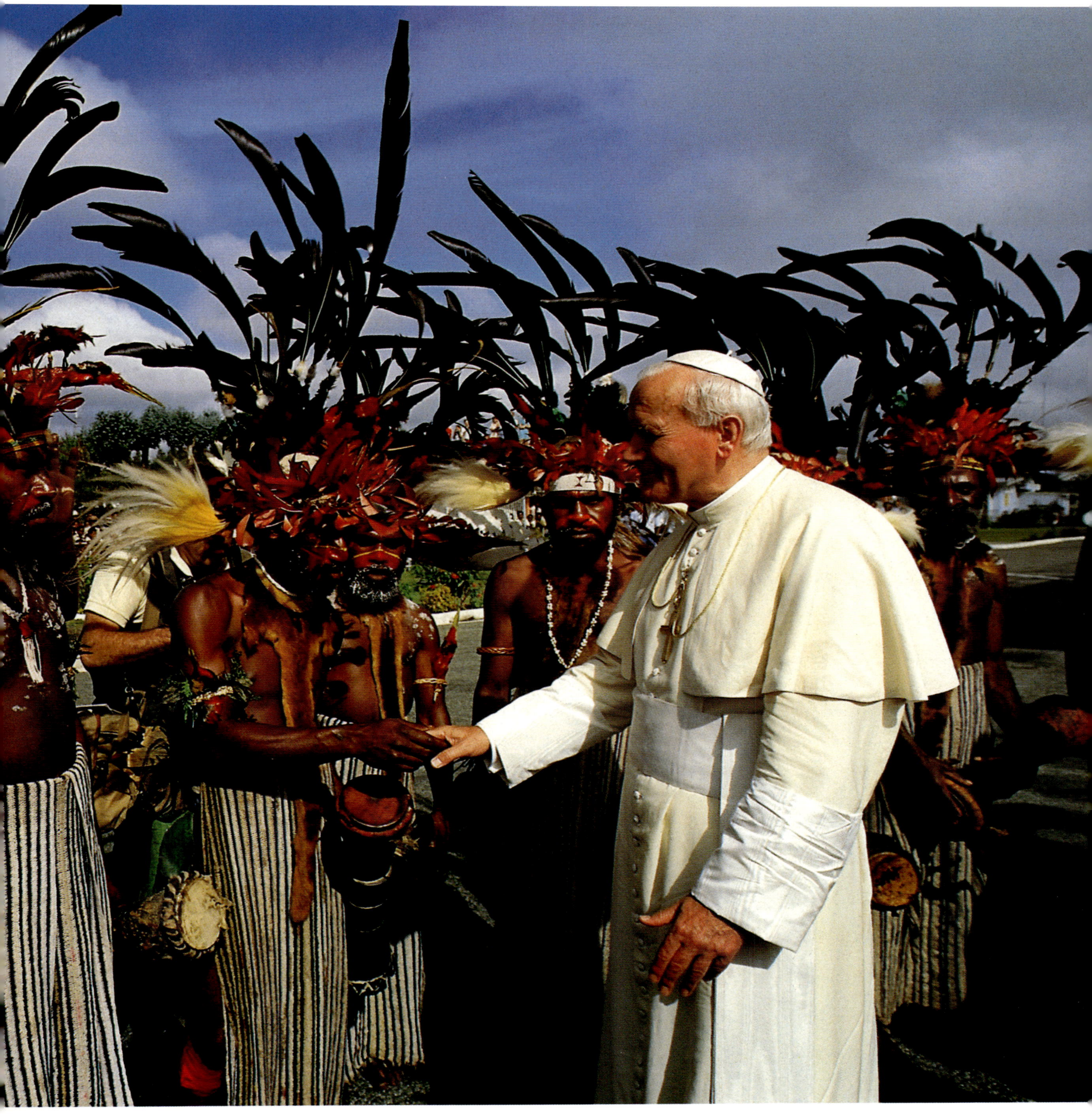

PHILIPPINES

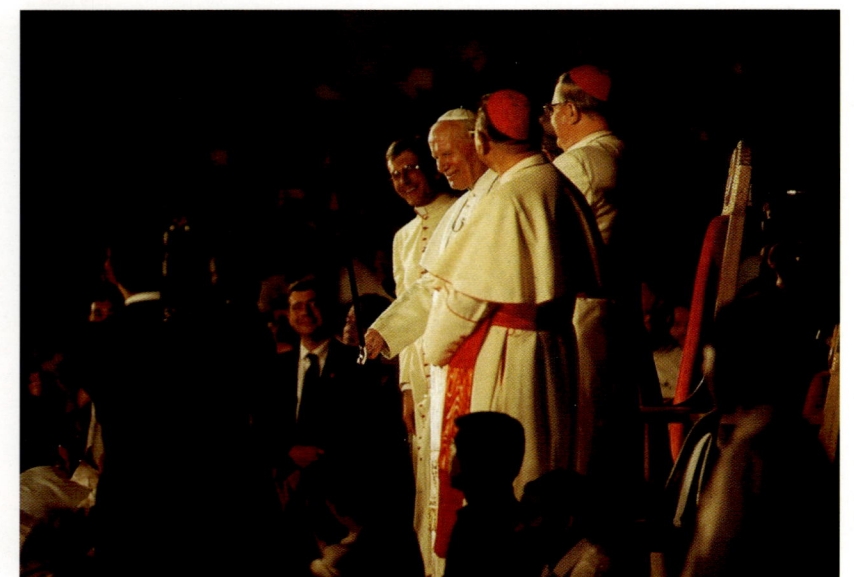

100-101 *Manila, 1995. John Paul II was not yet able to walk properly after his accident on April 29, 1994. Here he plays with his silver-topped cane, rolling it along the stage at his meeting with young people.*

102-103 *Manila, 1995. A huge crowd, three or perhaps four million people, attended the mass celebrated by the Pope. He closed the World Youth Day with these words: "Millions of young people are falling into covert, but real, forms of moral slavery."*

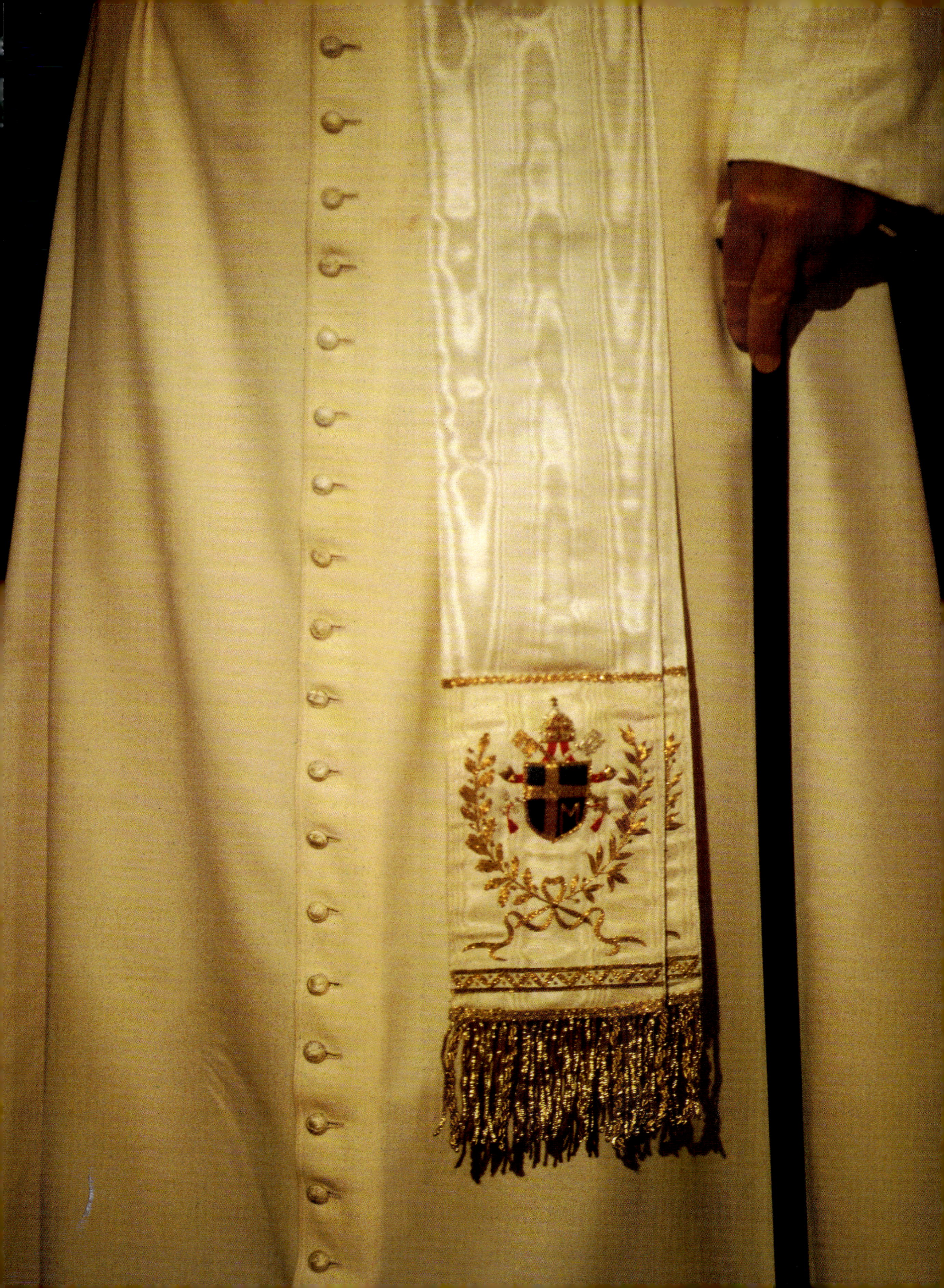

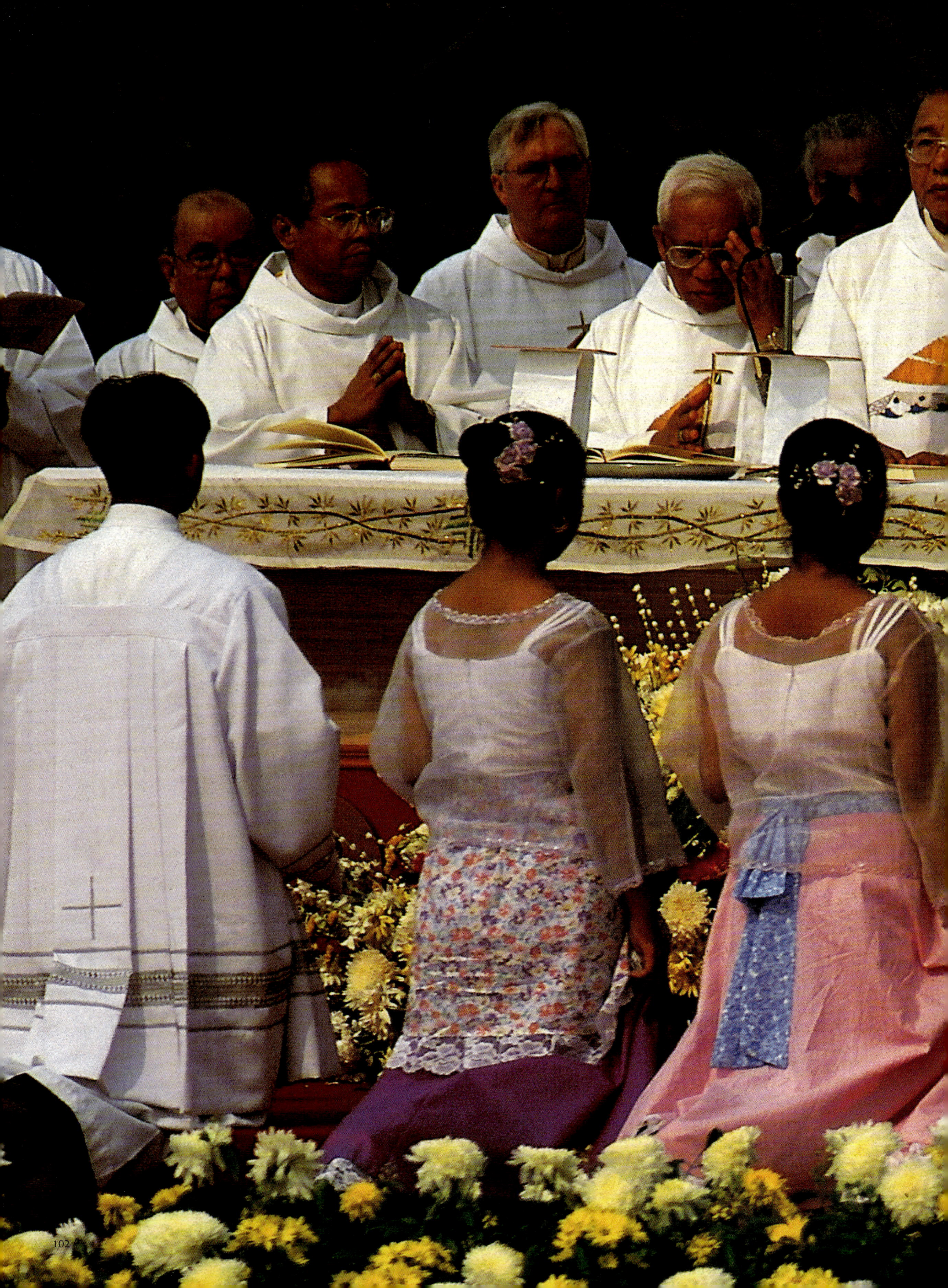

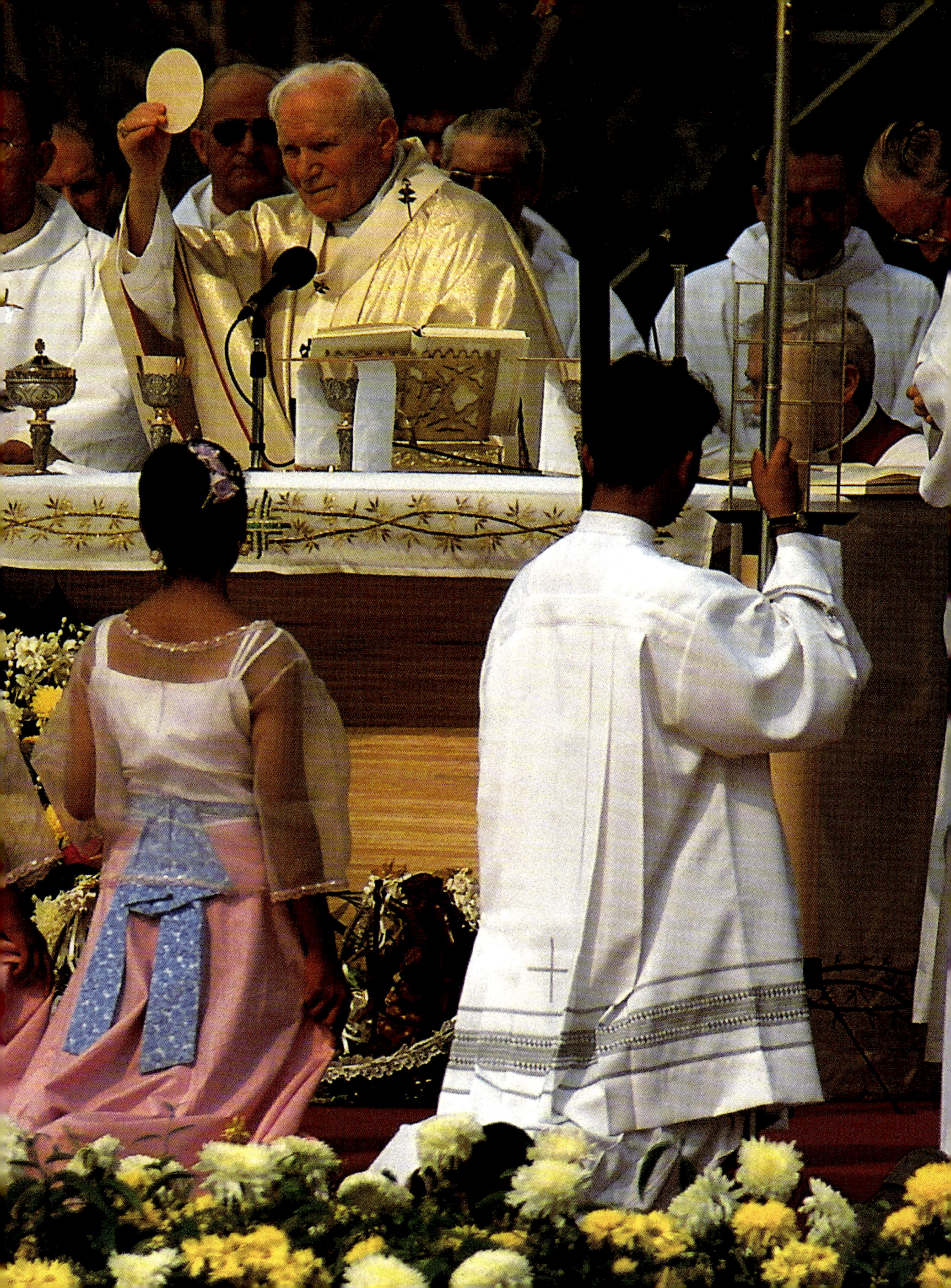

LITHUANIA

104-105 *Mass in Lithuania, 1993. After the election victory over the former Communists, the Pope delivered this warning: "It is very important that those who have lost remember that it is not enough simply to adjust to changed social conditions; it requires sincere conversion and, if necessary, expiation."*

106-107 *Vilnius, 1993. The Pope is momentarily overcome by emotion: "I also pray for all those who have no cross on their graves."*

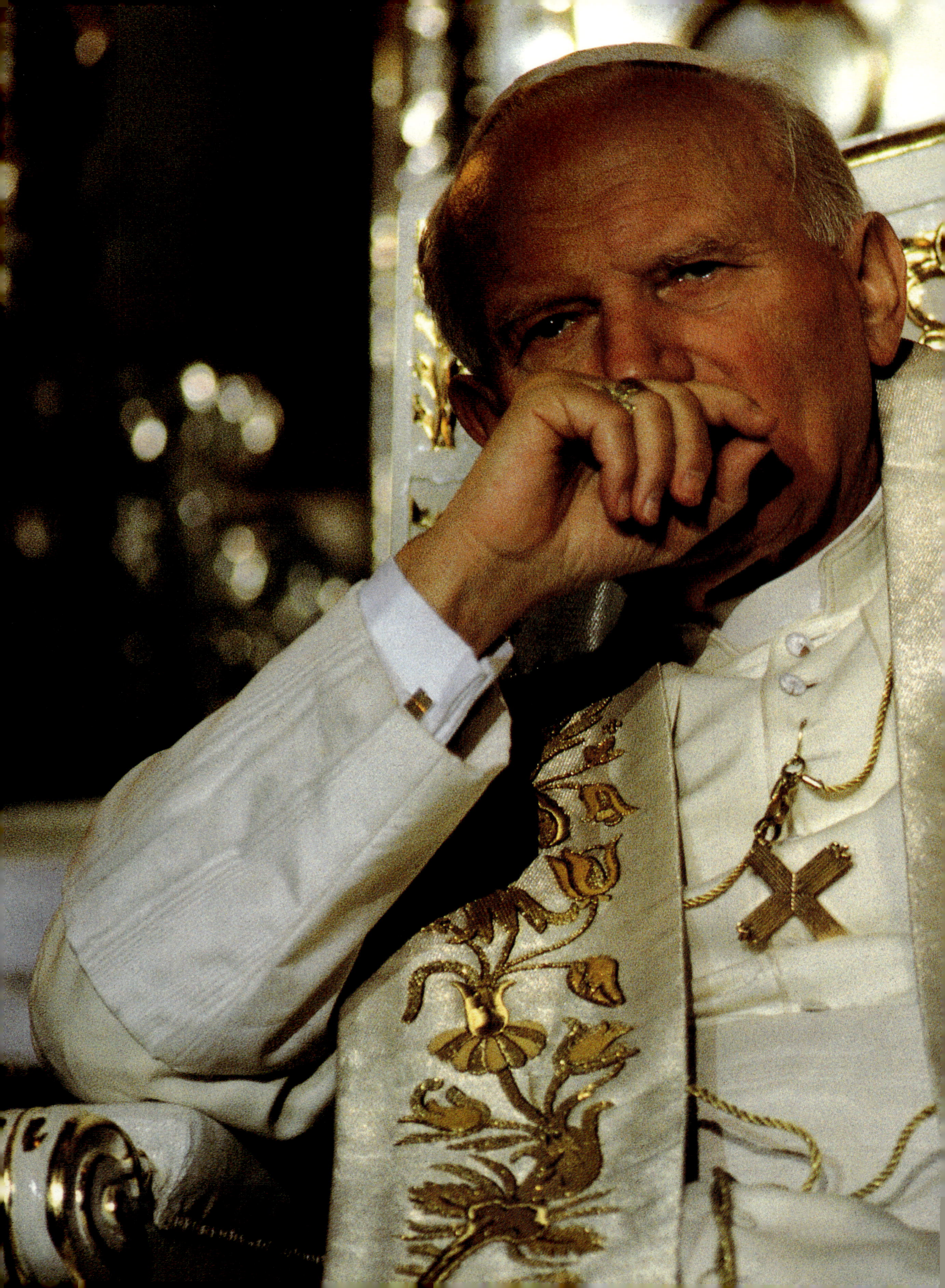

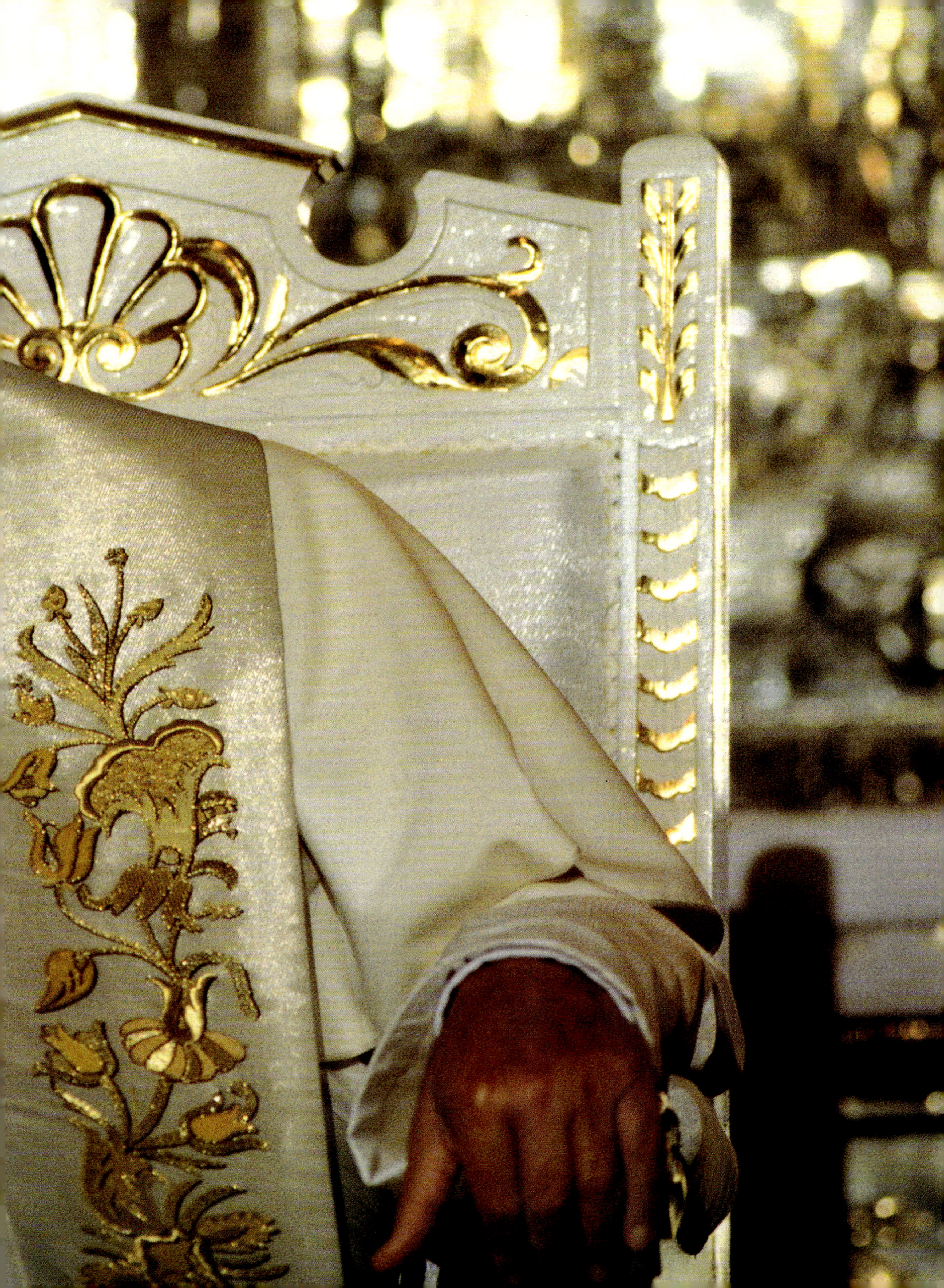

PORTUGAL

108-109 Lisbon, 1982. A measureless crowd welcomed Karol Wojtyla at Fatima, where he gave thanks to the Madonna for saving his life from the assassin's bullet the previous year.

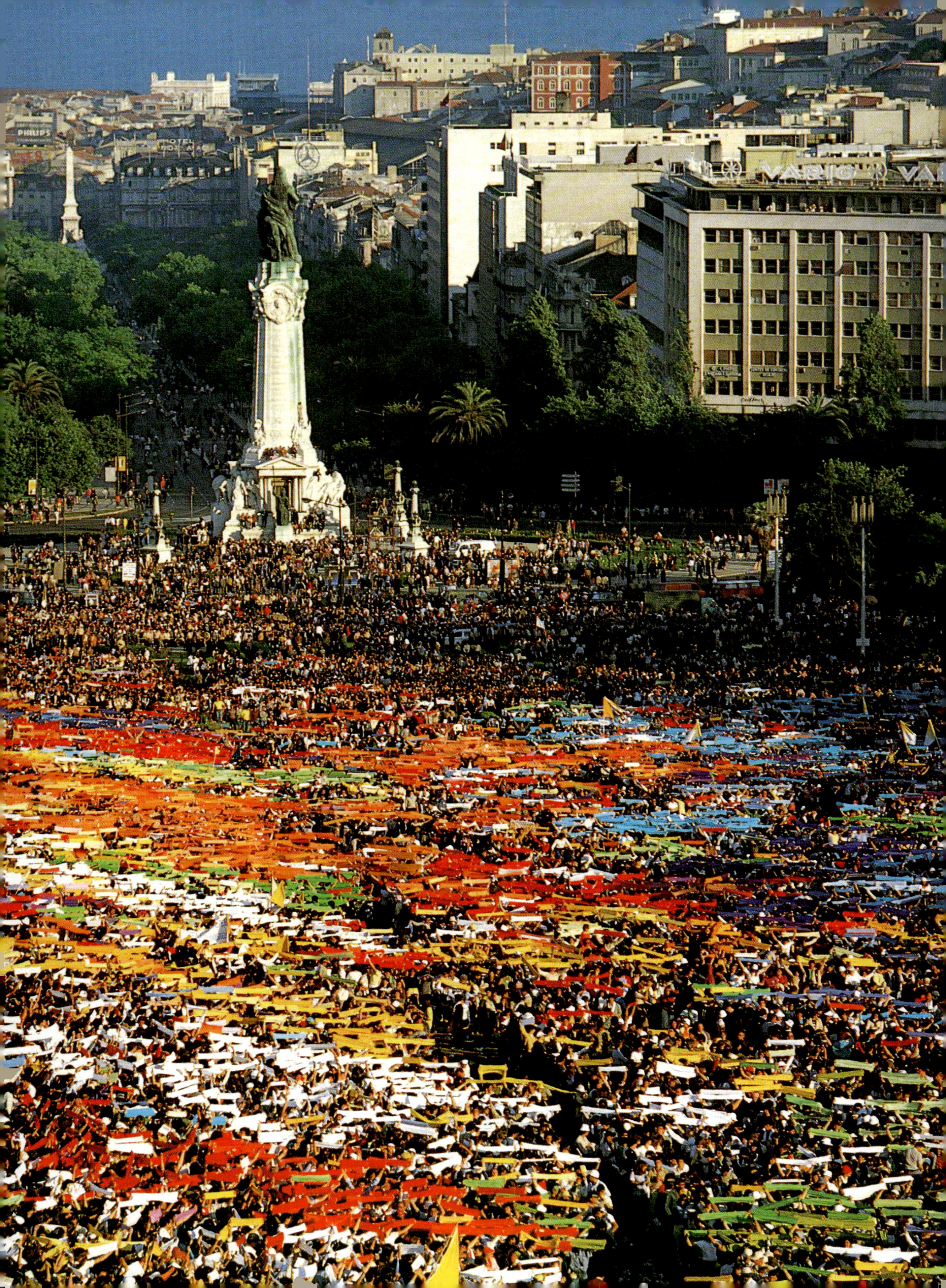
PHILIPS
VARIG

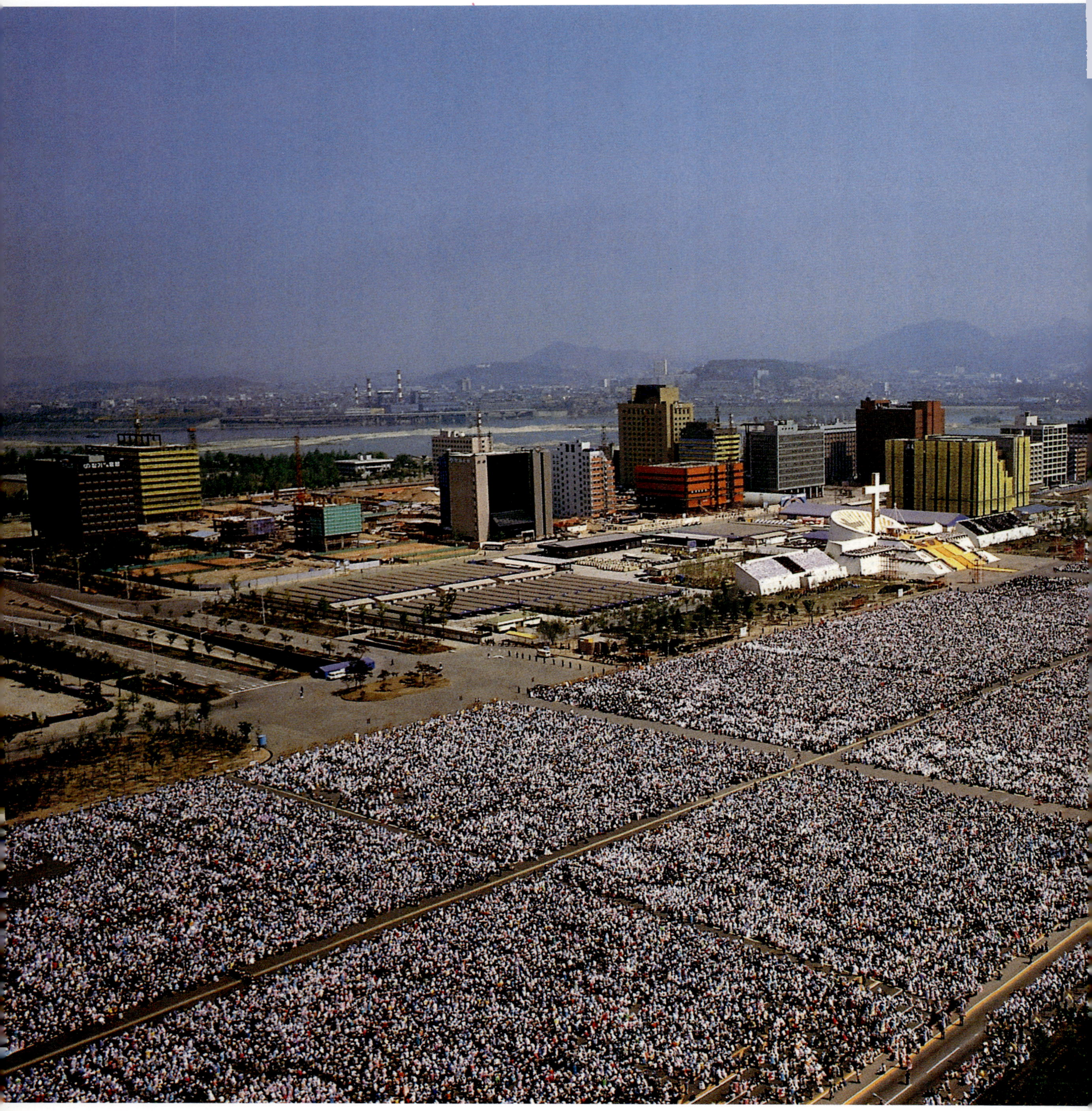

SOUTH KOREA

110-111 *Seoul, 1984. John Paul II's visit was immensely important for Korean Roman Catholics. The Pope prayed for the country's unification in front of a crowd of one million people: "May your beloved country, which has been tragically divided into two parts for more than a generation, be reunited as one family."*

FRANCE

112 August 1983, the Pope at Lourdes. He celebrated mass near the Grotto, before an audience of two hundred thousand pilgrims on the field and the hill opposite the sanctuary.

113 Lourdes, 1983. The Pope prays in the Grotto: "I have become a pilgrim and my day here with you will be a simple one, just like any other pilgrim's."

114-115 Lourdes, 1983. To young people: "We love the Church too. How we should love it to be more transparent, freer from all kinds of compromise!"

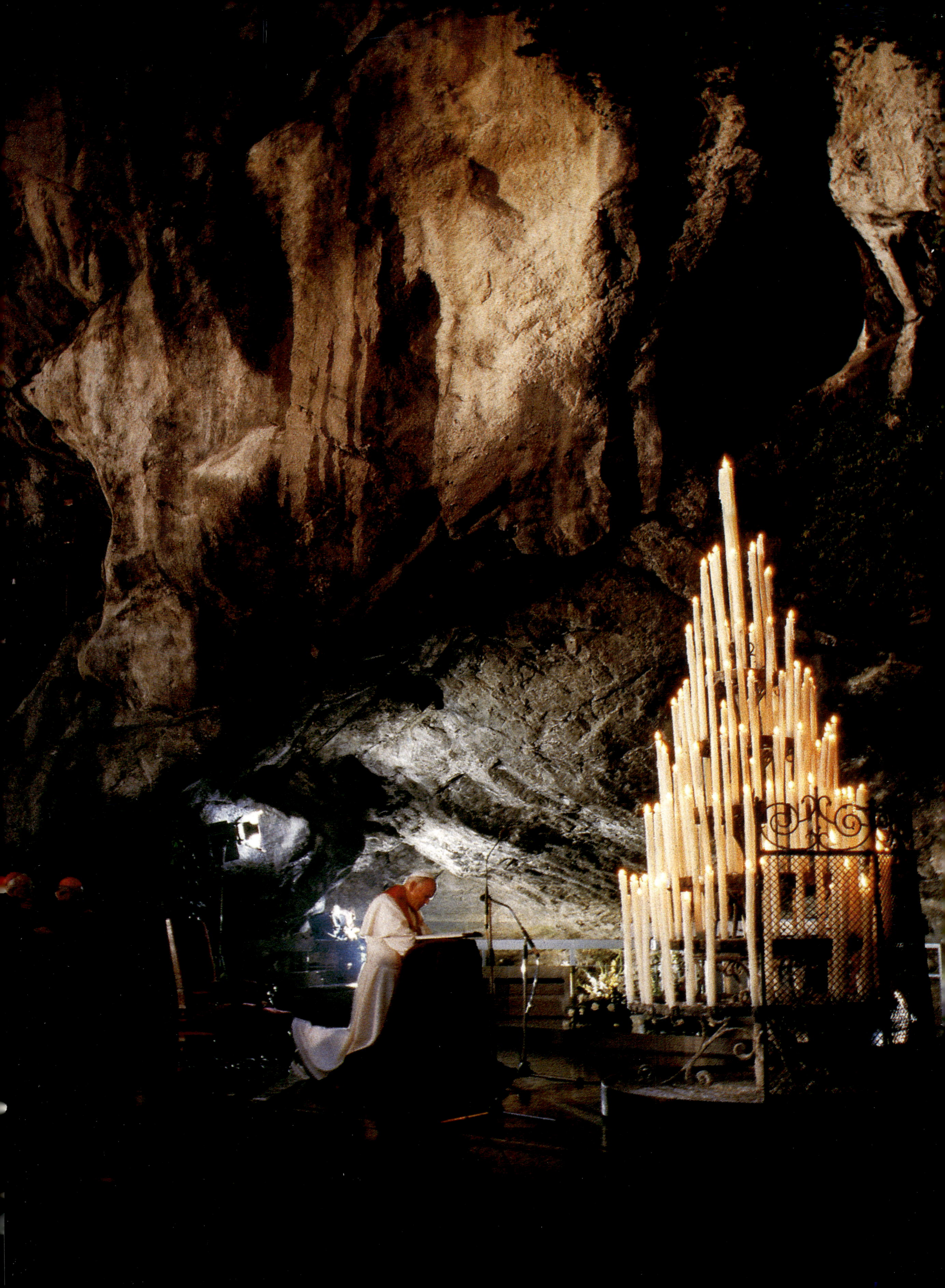

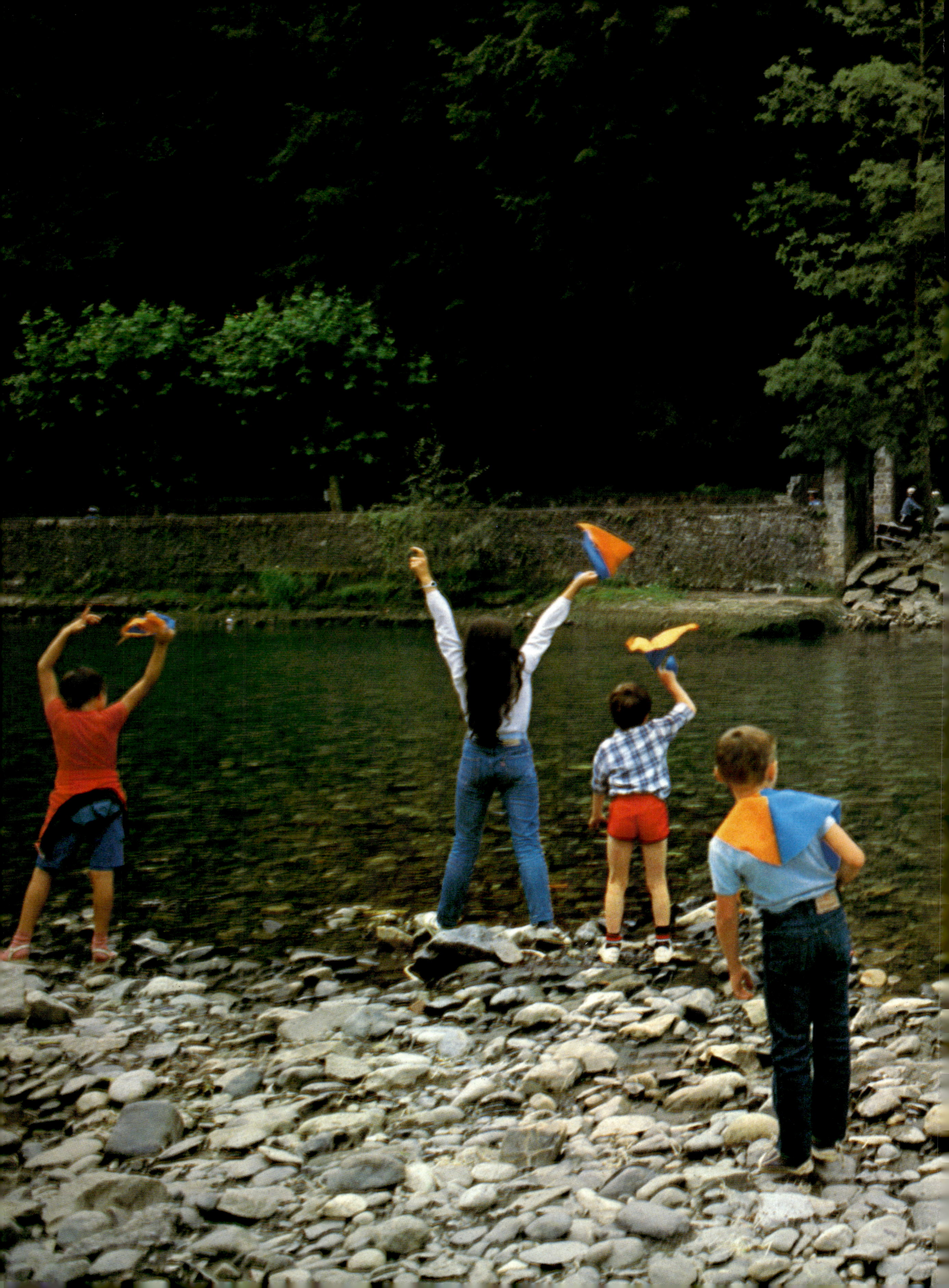

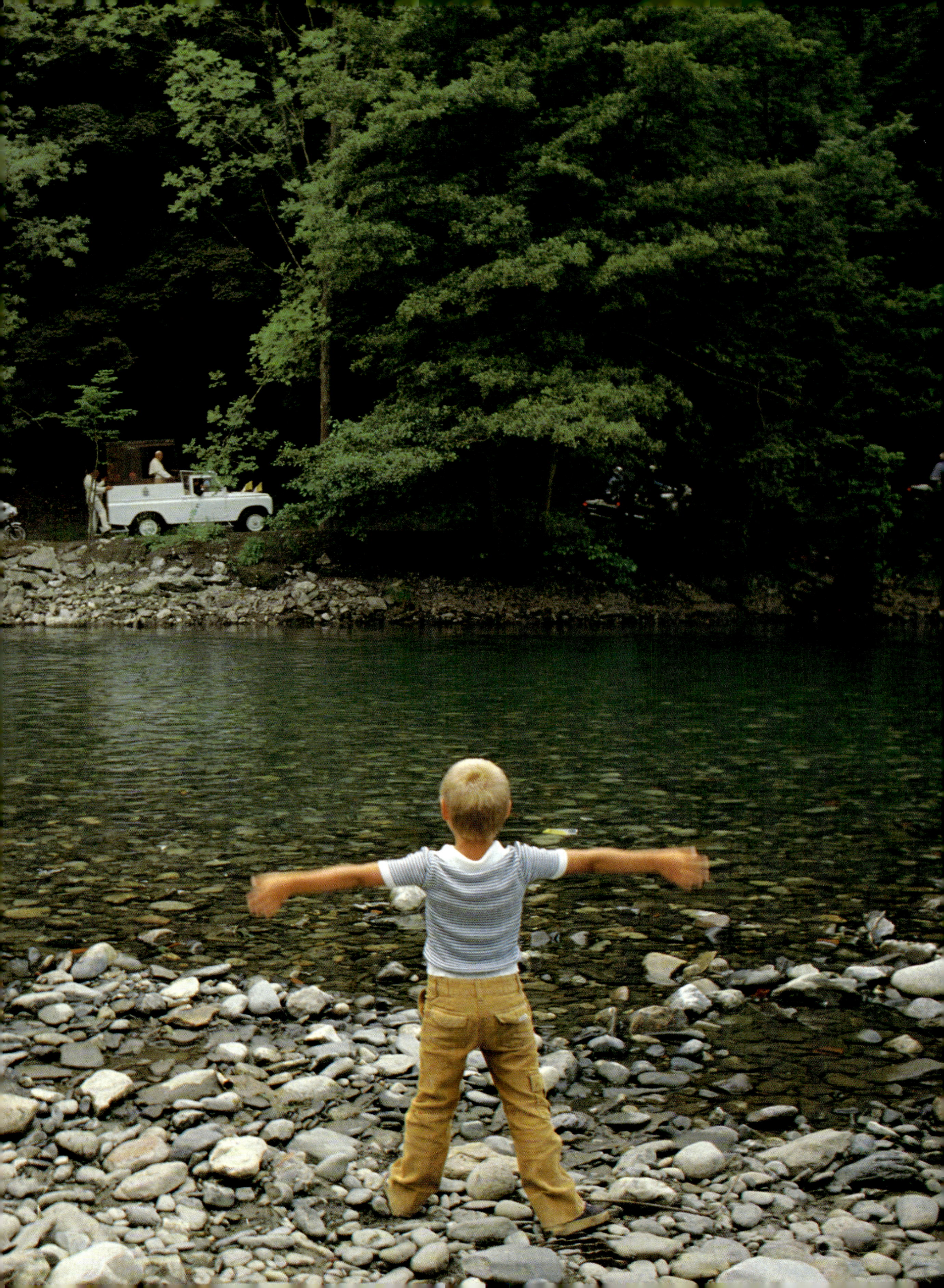

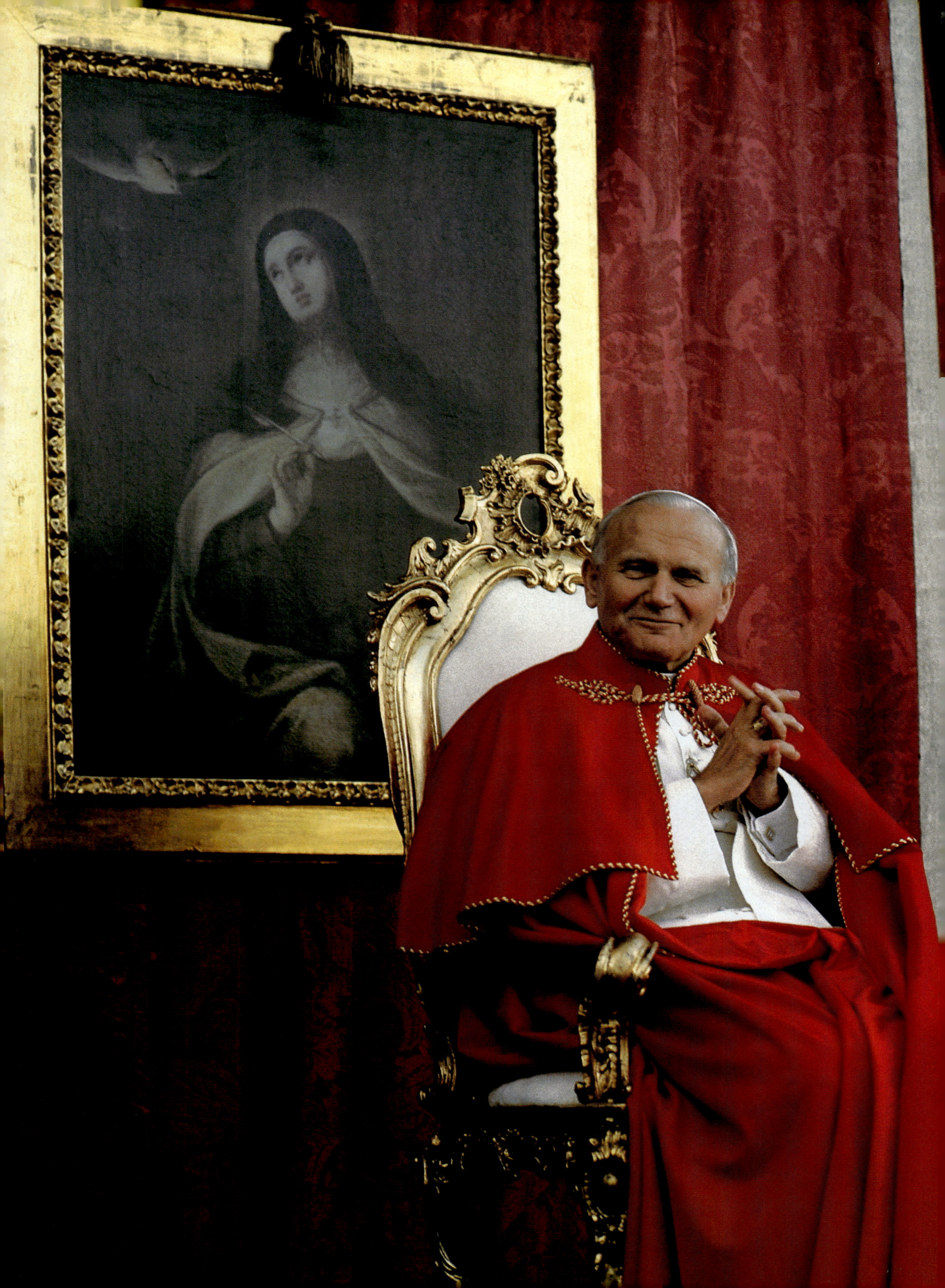

SPAIN

116-117 *Avila, 1982. One of the Pope's most triumphant journeys in Europe, during which he admitted that "times like those of the Inquisition produced tensions, errors, and excesses."*

118-119 *Guadalupe, 1982. Christians "must let their voices be heard while at the same time respecting the beliefs of others, in accordance with the values in which they believe."*

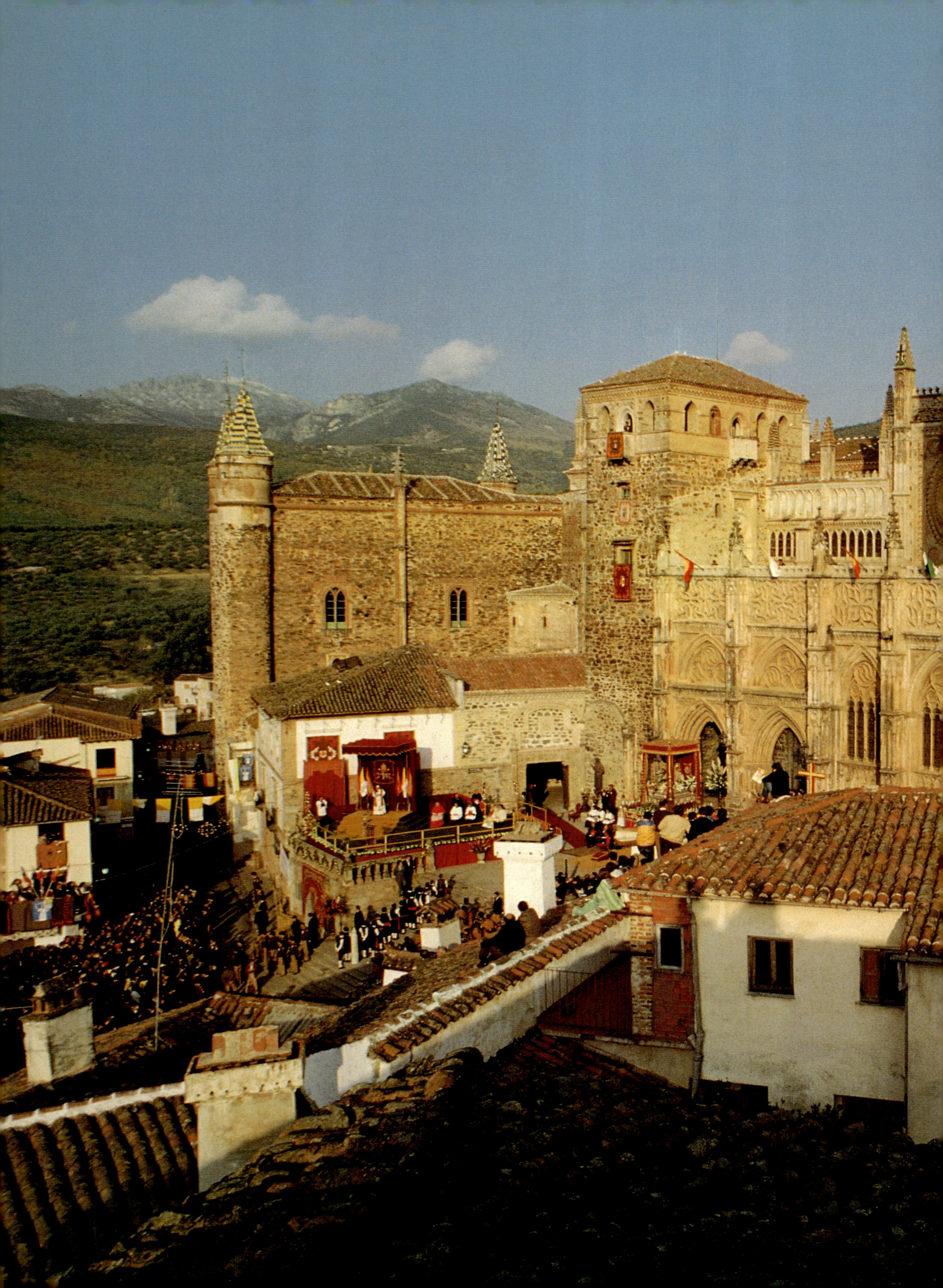

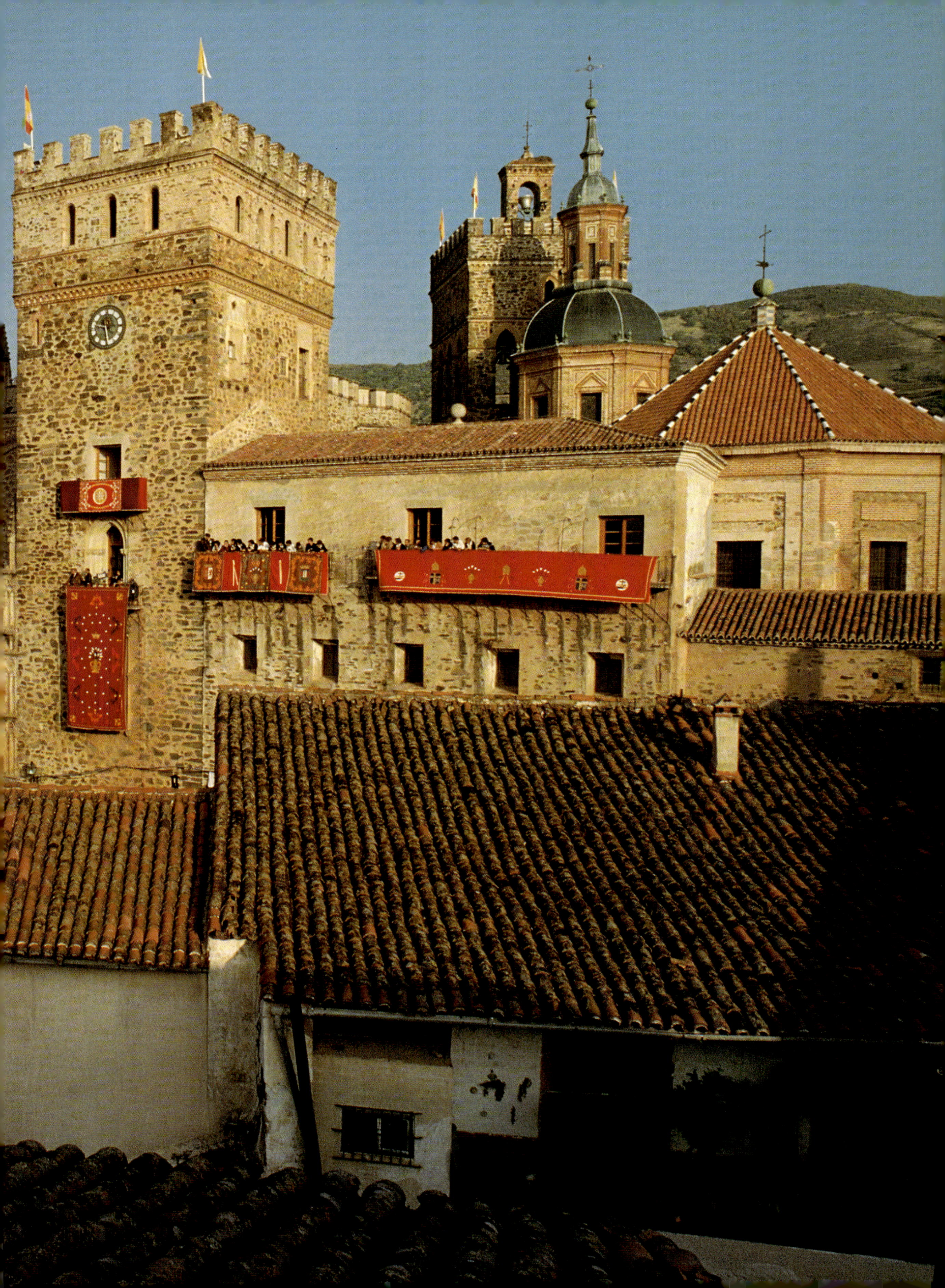

120-121 *In May 1982, during the Falklands War, the Pope visited the United Kingdom. Here the "Popemobile" travels through the streets of London.*

UNITED KINGDOM

121 (top) *London, 1982. The papal procession moves past Big Ben. This was the first time that a Pope had stepped onto English soil since the Anglican schism. For the first time the Pope was welcomed as a spiritual leader and not a head of state: without gun salutes, national anthems, or military honor guards.*

121 (bottom) *Liverpool, 1982. John Paul II's visit to the United Kingdom during the war with Argentina was greeted with increasing warmth the farther north he went.*

SAN SALVADOR

122 *San Salvador, March 1983. Armed soldiers escorted the Pope wherever he went. Bishop Rivera y Damas welcomed him with these words: "The horror of an absurd tragedy is hanging over our people. Holy Father, Christ suffers here in our brothers."*

123 *San Salvador, 1983. The Pope prays on the grave of Monsignor Oscar Romero, killed by right-wing extremists while he celebrated mass.*

SABIAS QUE LLEGARIA
LA MUERTE SIN AVISAR
PERO LA MUERTE ES SEMILLA

GERMANY

124 *Mainz, 1980. Pope John Paul II in prayer at the grave of Bishop Kettler, an advocate for the social rights of workers and immigrants.*

125 *Cologne, 1980. John Paul II visited Germany for the first time since being elected Pope. After a service in the splendid cathedral at Cologne, he met university staff and students and spoke about science and faith, admitting the mistakes made at the time of Galileo: "The Church remembers this with regret; today we are aware of the mistakes and the shortcomings of such procedures."*

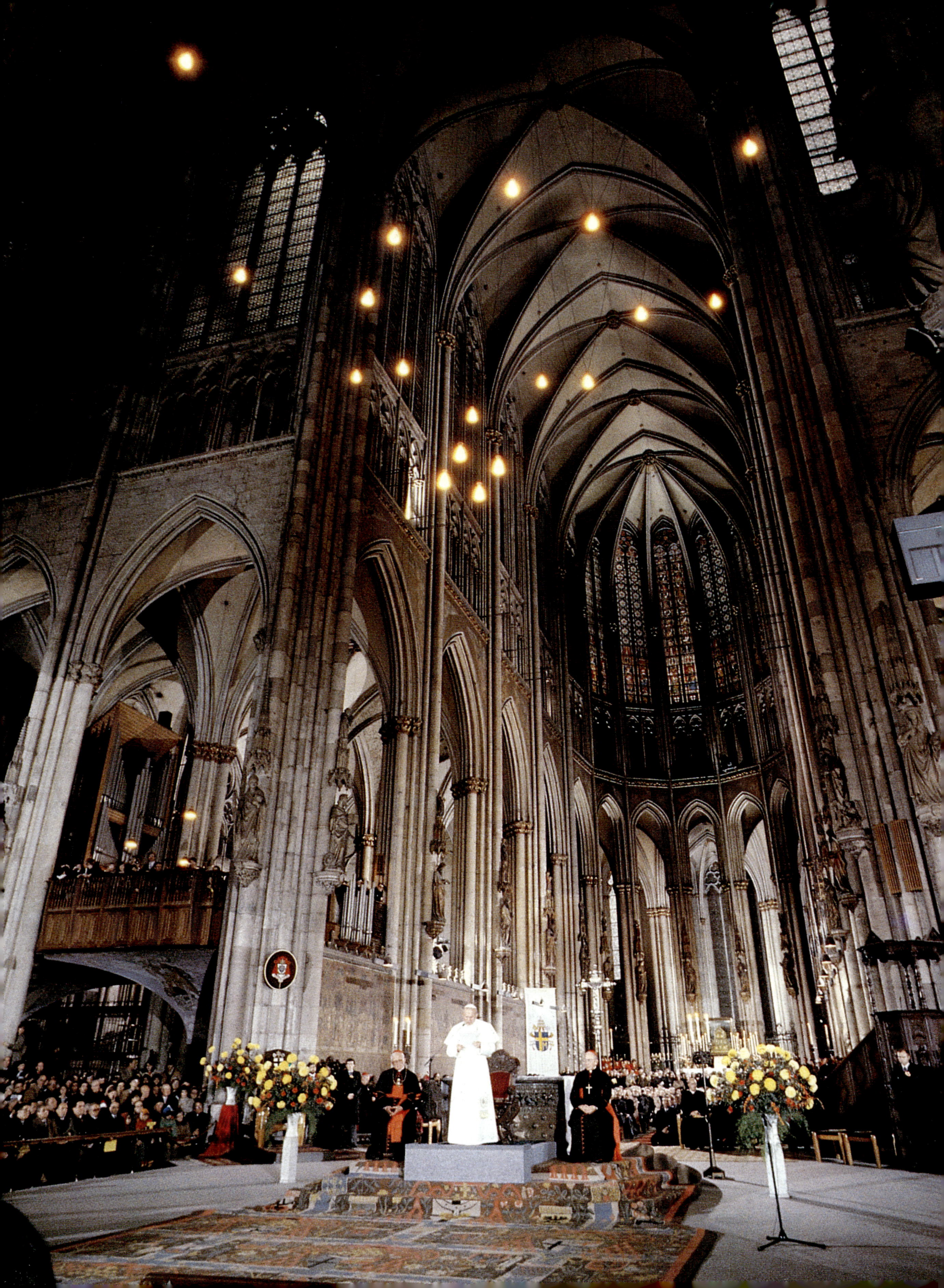

126 *Fulda, 1980. "Ecumenism is an urgent task" — the words of John Paul II in the land of Martin Luther.*

127 *Mainz, 1980. During an important ecumenical conference, John Paul II recognized reciprocal responsibilities at the time of the Reformation: "We all need conversion, we want to recognize that we have made mistakes."*

NICARAGUA

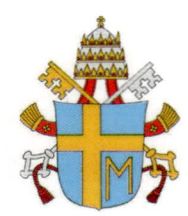

128 Managua, March 1983. Welcoming crowds greet the Pope on his arrival in Nicaragua.

128-129 Managua, March 1983. The Pope addresses a crowd in front of a portrait of Sandino. This was the first time that John Paul II faced a hostile demonstration during mass. His condemnation of the pro-regime "populist church" was greeted with shouts and whistles from the regime's supporters in the crowd.

129

BRAZIL

130-131 *Bahia San Salvador, Brazil, 1980. John Paul II visits the favelas. "Land is a gift from God, to all human beings."*

131

132 *Rio de Janeiro, July 1980. Numerous pilgrims attend John Paul II's mass at the sanctuary of the Aparecida.*

132-133 *Rio de Janeiro, July 1980. The Pope returns to the nunciature after addressing a gathering of almost two million people. "It was the biggest crowd ever in Brazil," according to the headlines in the press.*

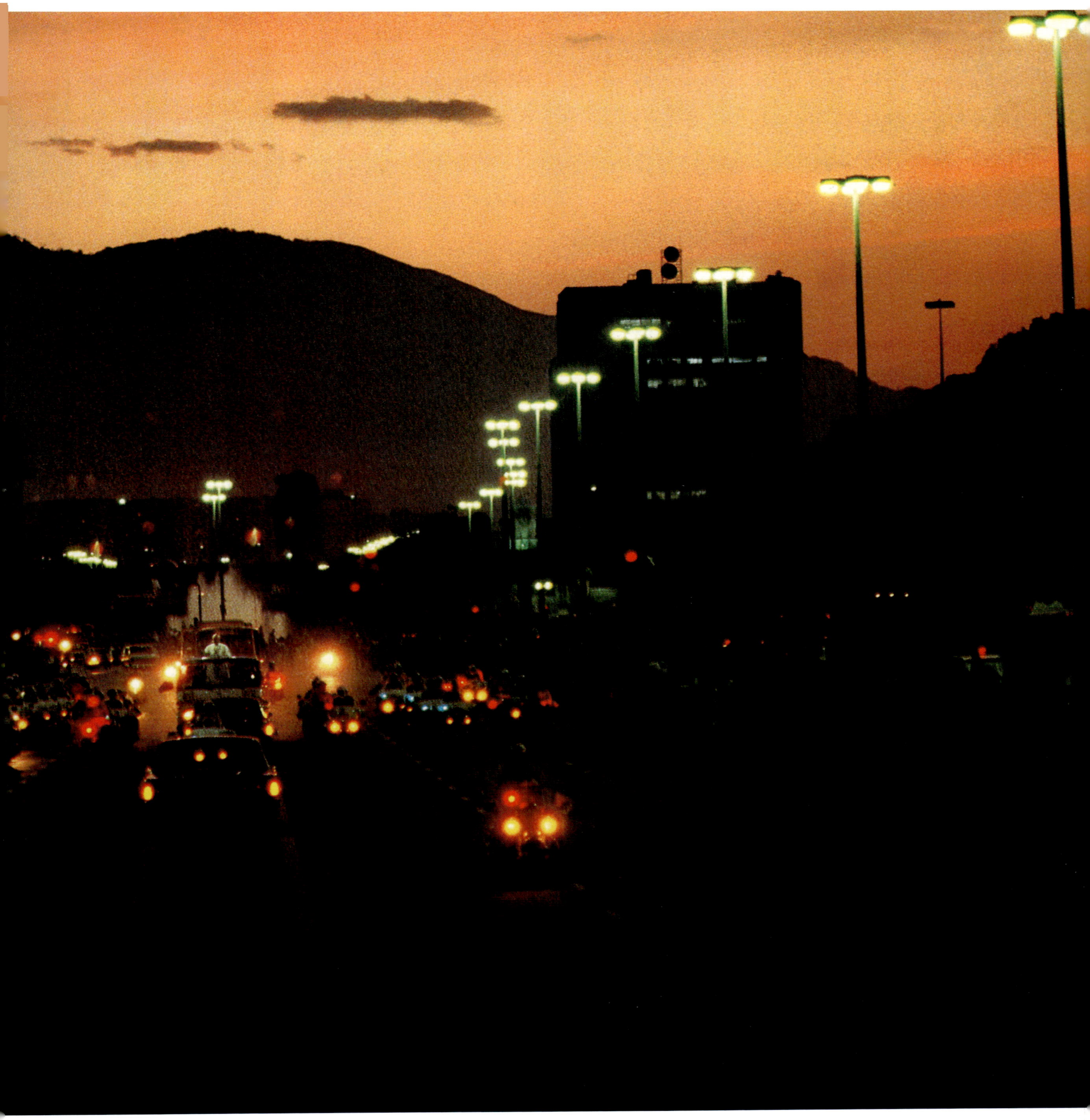

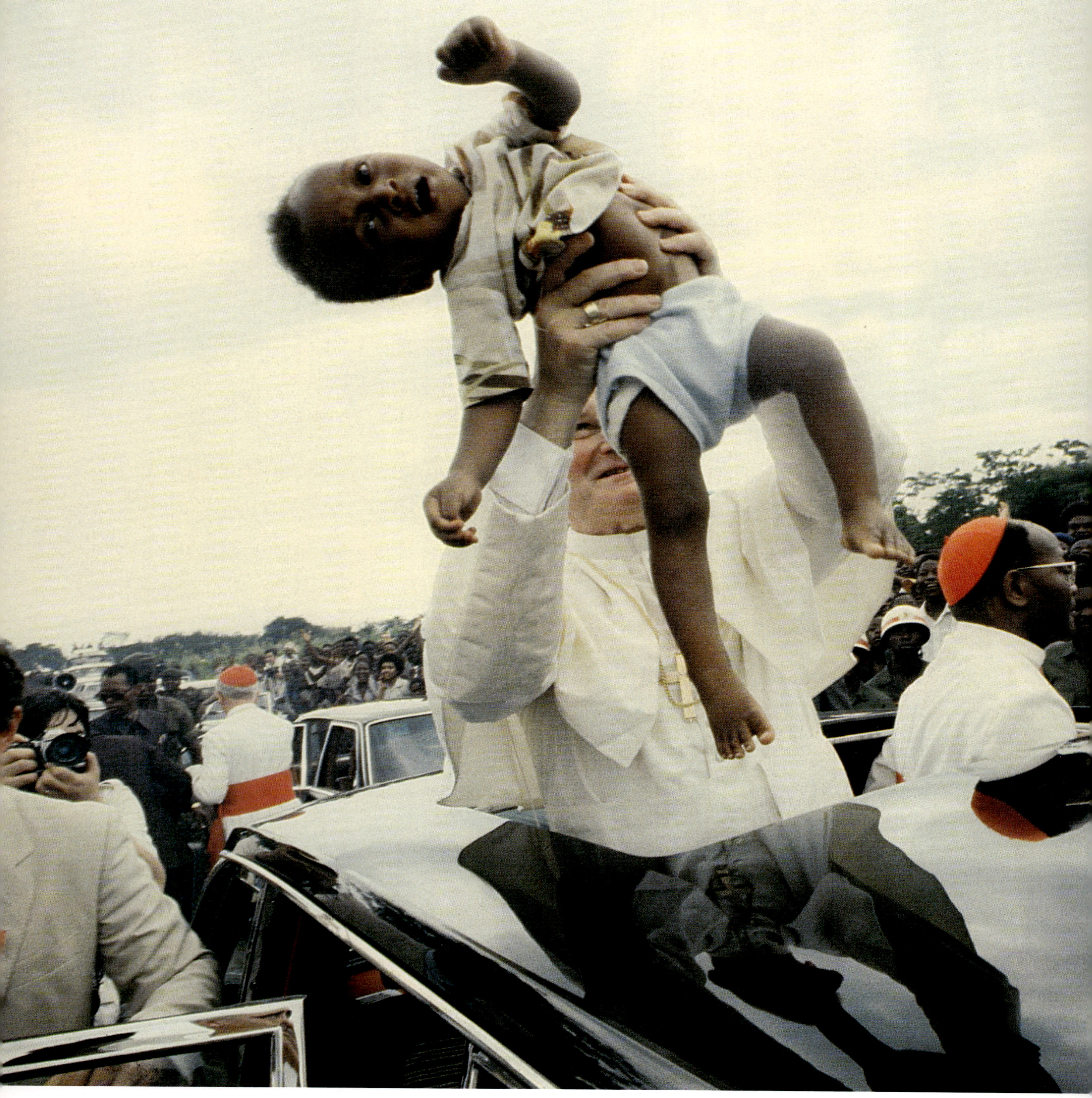

ZAIRE

134-135 *Kinshasa, Zaire, May 1980. John Paul II celebrating the centenary of the first Roman Catholic church in the country. A huge crowd awaited the Pope, who spoke of the "scourge of racism."*

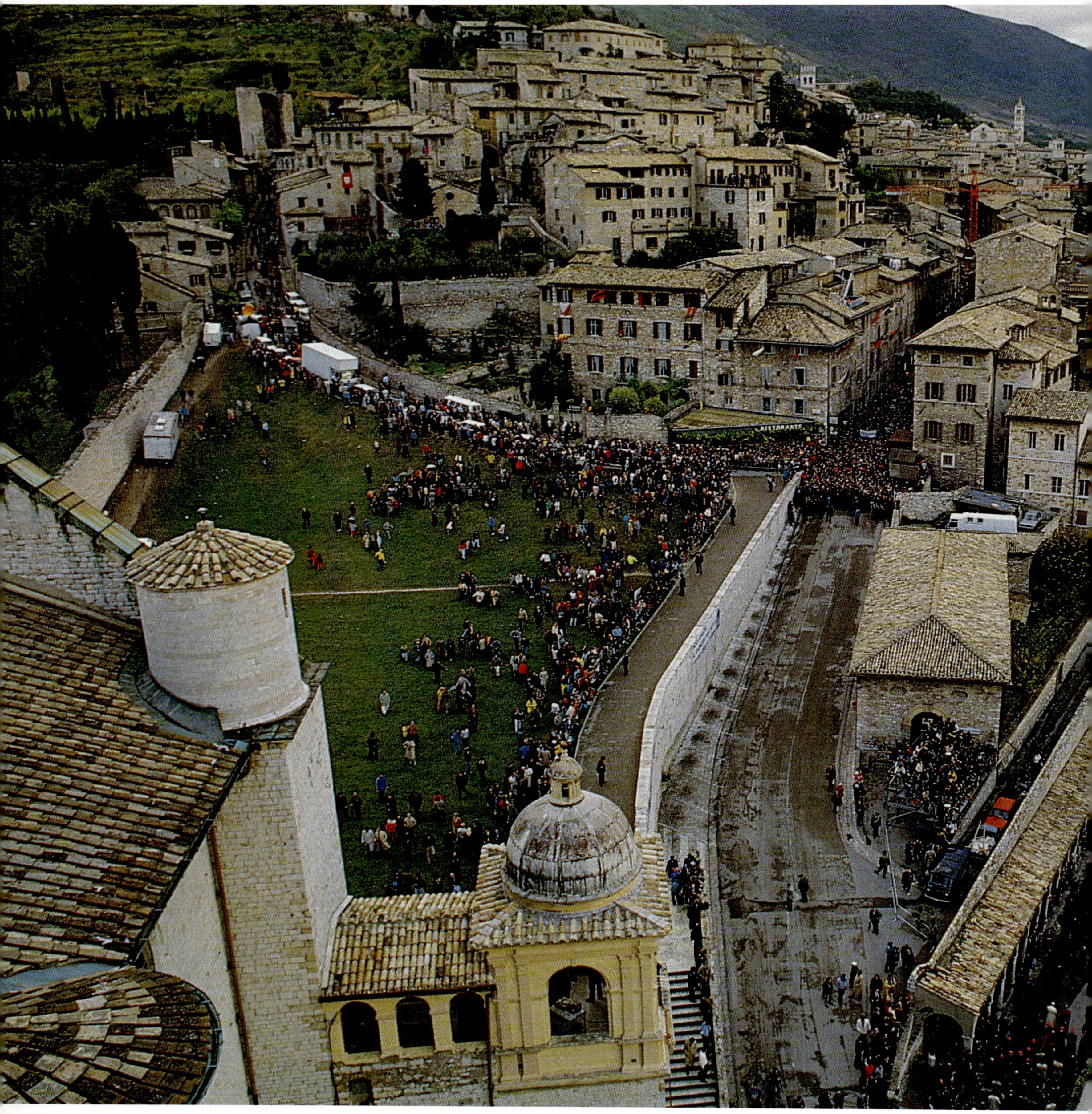

ITALY

136-137 *Assisi, city of peace, November 1986. Representatives of all the world's main religions accepted the Pope's invitation to meet in Assisi for a joint day of prayer.*

137 (top) *The Pope climbs up toward the basilica of St. Francis at Assisi.*

137 (bottom) *The Pope at prayer during the meeting at Assisi.*

138 Venice, June 1985. John Paul II in a gondola on the Grand Canal.

139 Nuoro, October 1985. A moment of rest, or meditation, during a meeting with townspeople.

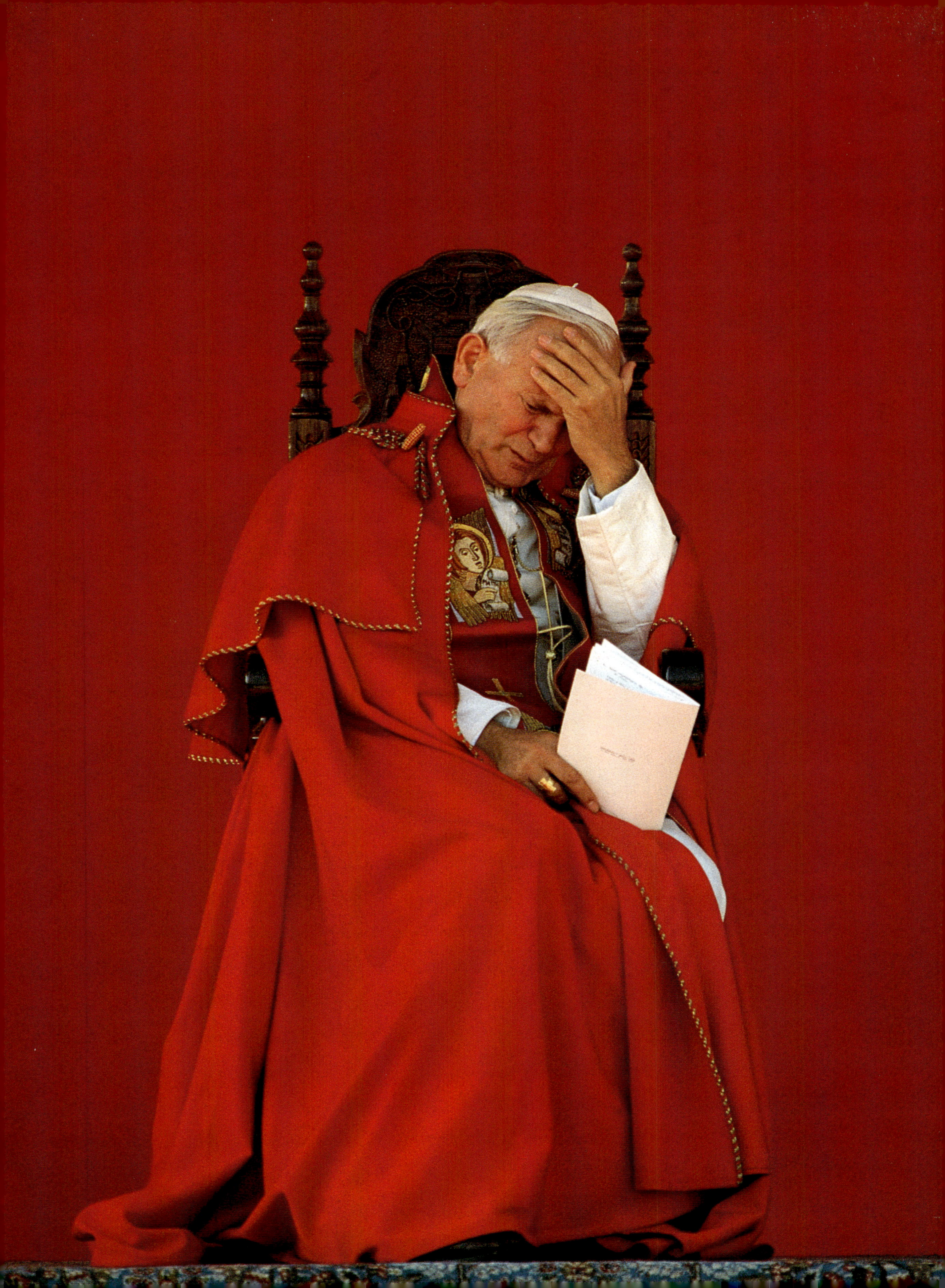

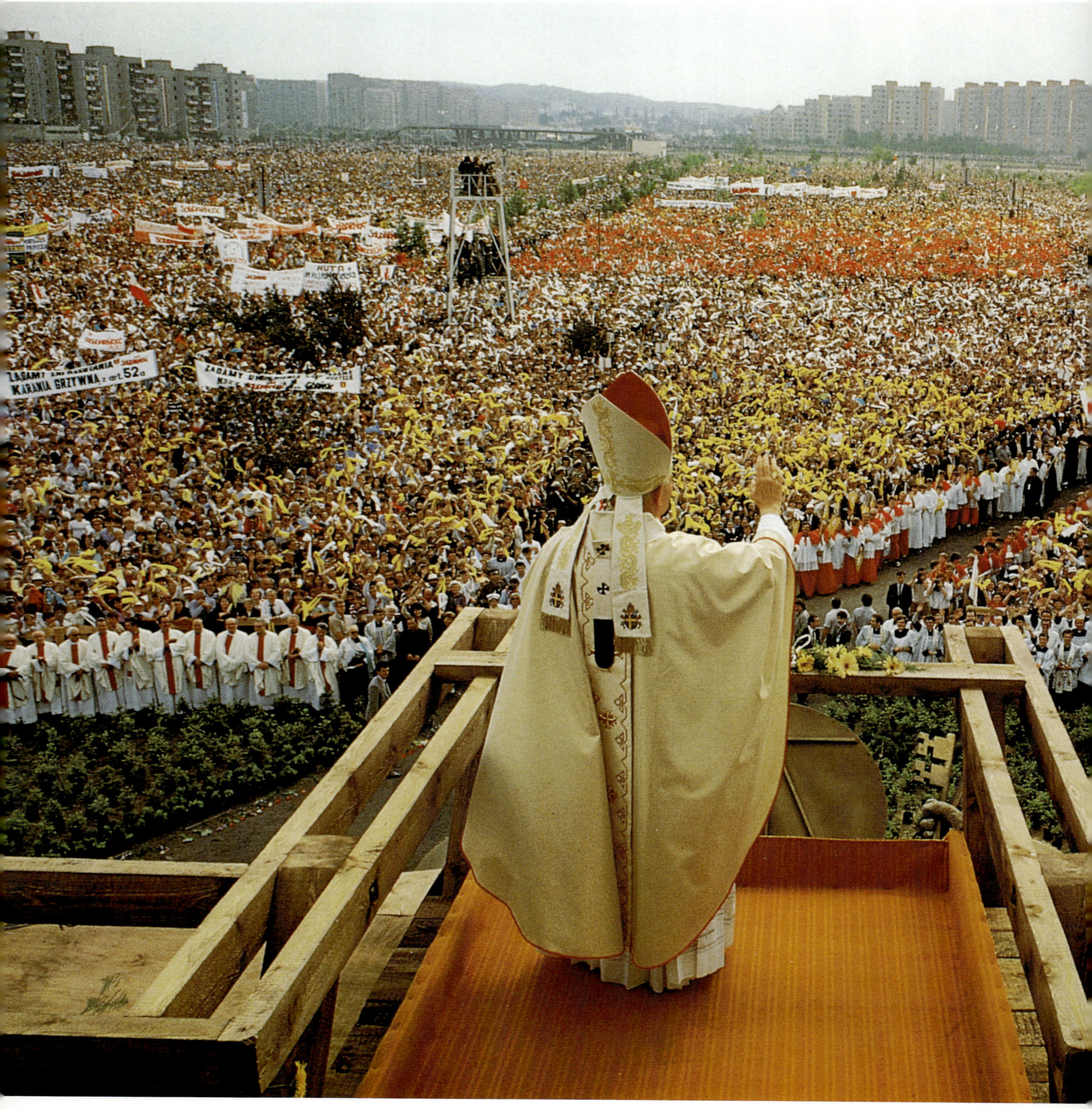
HUTA
KARANIA GRZYWNA z art. 52a

POLAND

140-141 *Gdansk, 1987. The Pope went back to Poland in 1987 and visited Gdansk (it had not been possible in 1983). He praised the free trade union, Solidarity: "This word has been pronounced in a new way and a new context here, and the world cannot forget it."*

141 (top) *Tarnow, 1987. The "Pope's Divisions": Polish priests follow the celebration of mass.*

141 (bottom) *Katowice, 1983. Mass is celebrated under torrential rain. The Pope defends trade union freedom before a huge crowd. "No one confers this right, it is an innate right."*

CANADA

142 (top) *Yellow Knife, September 1984. A gift for the Pope: a richly decorated and embroidered Huron jacket.*

142 (bottom) *Toronto, September 1984. Preparations for the Pope's mass. "Attempts to substitute something else for God are all in vain. Nothing can fill the vacuum which He leaves."*

142-143 *Yellow Knife, September 1984. Pope John Paul II in a tepee belonging to Huron Indians. "History provides clear proof that over the centuries your people have been the repeated victims of injustice from new arrivals."*

143

UNITED STATES OF AMERICA

144 *U.N., New York, 5 October 1995*
Cardinal John O'Connor kneels before the Holy Father.

144-145 *U.N., New York, October 5, 1995.*
John Paul II addresses the General Assembly of the United Nations at its headquarters. He urged the U.N. to write a "Declaration of the Rights of Nations," so that "we may realize that the tears of this century have watered the ground in preparation for a new spring for the spirit."

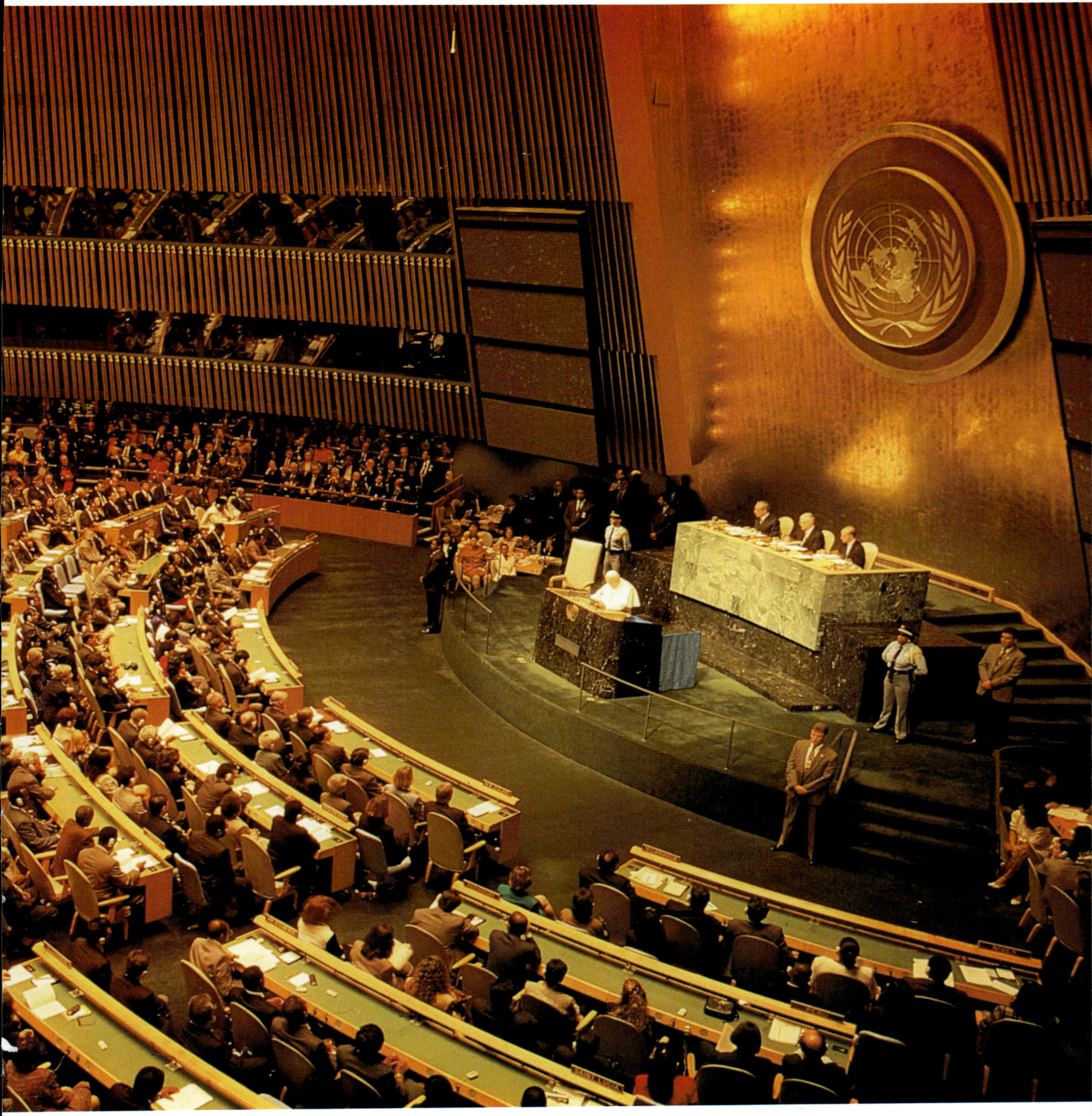

146 and 147 *Baltimore, U.S.A., October 1995. At the end of his trip, John Paul II appealed to the United States to "defend the right to life, from its conception to its natural end, to look after and defend the unborn and all those who might otherwise be seen by others as a nuisance or undesirable."*

148-149 *New York, U.S.A., October 1995. The high spot of the Pope's New York trip was the great mass in Central Park. In the heart of the city symbolizing wealth, the Pope said: "You are called upon to 'see to' the needs of the poor, the hungry, the homeless, and all those who are alone or ill: those suffering from AIDS, for example."*

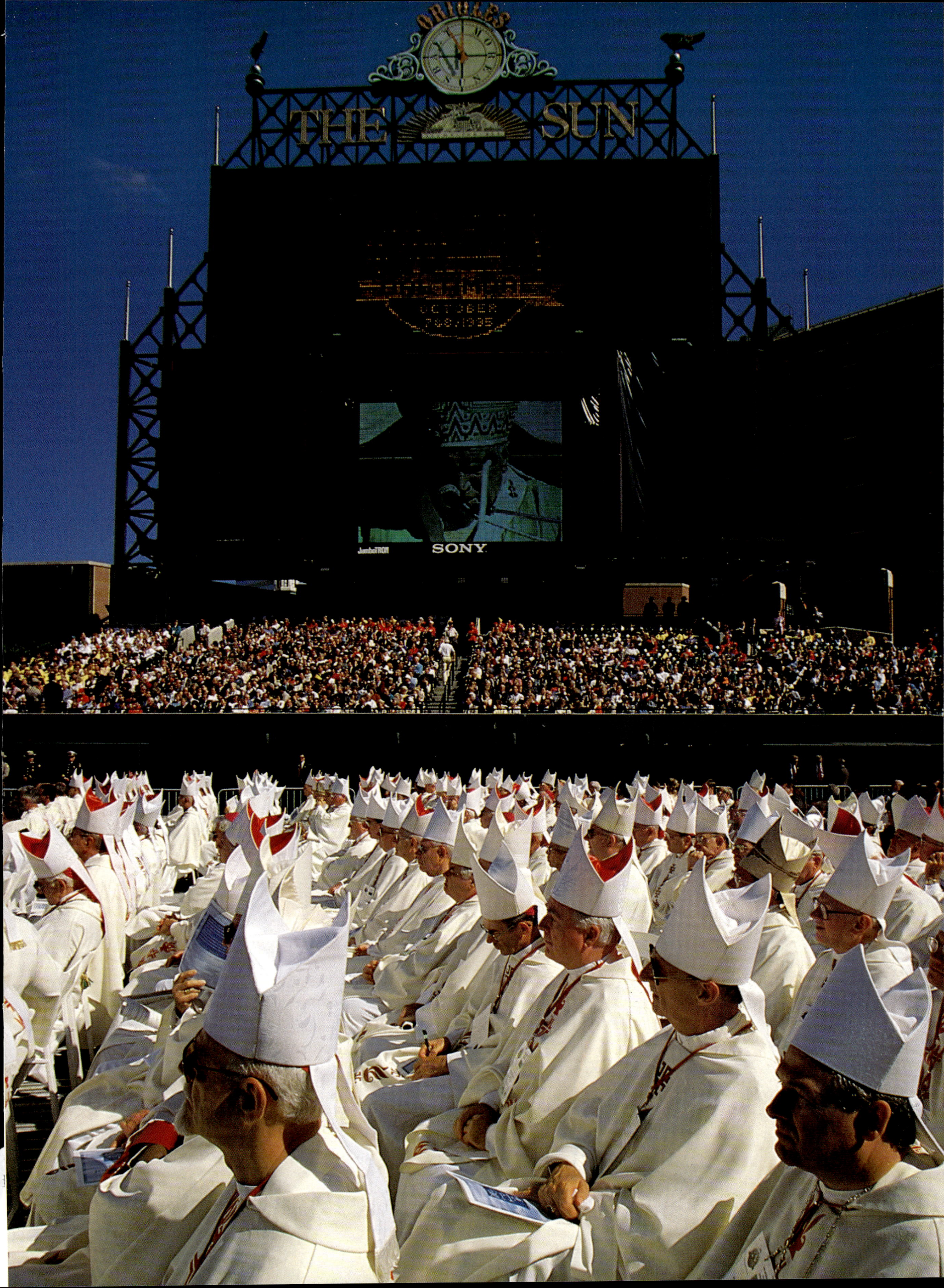
ORIOLES
THE SUN
OCTOBER
SONY

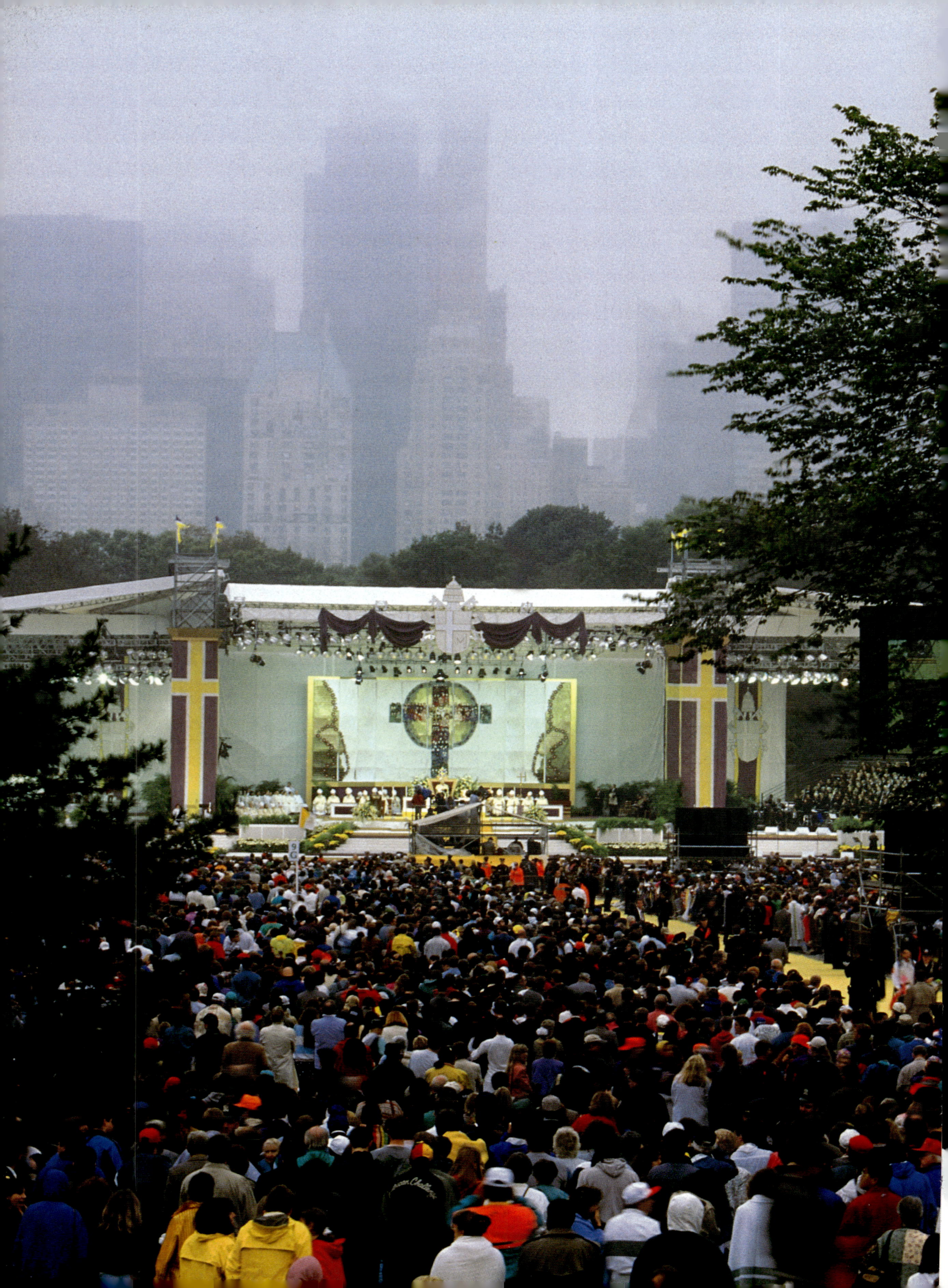

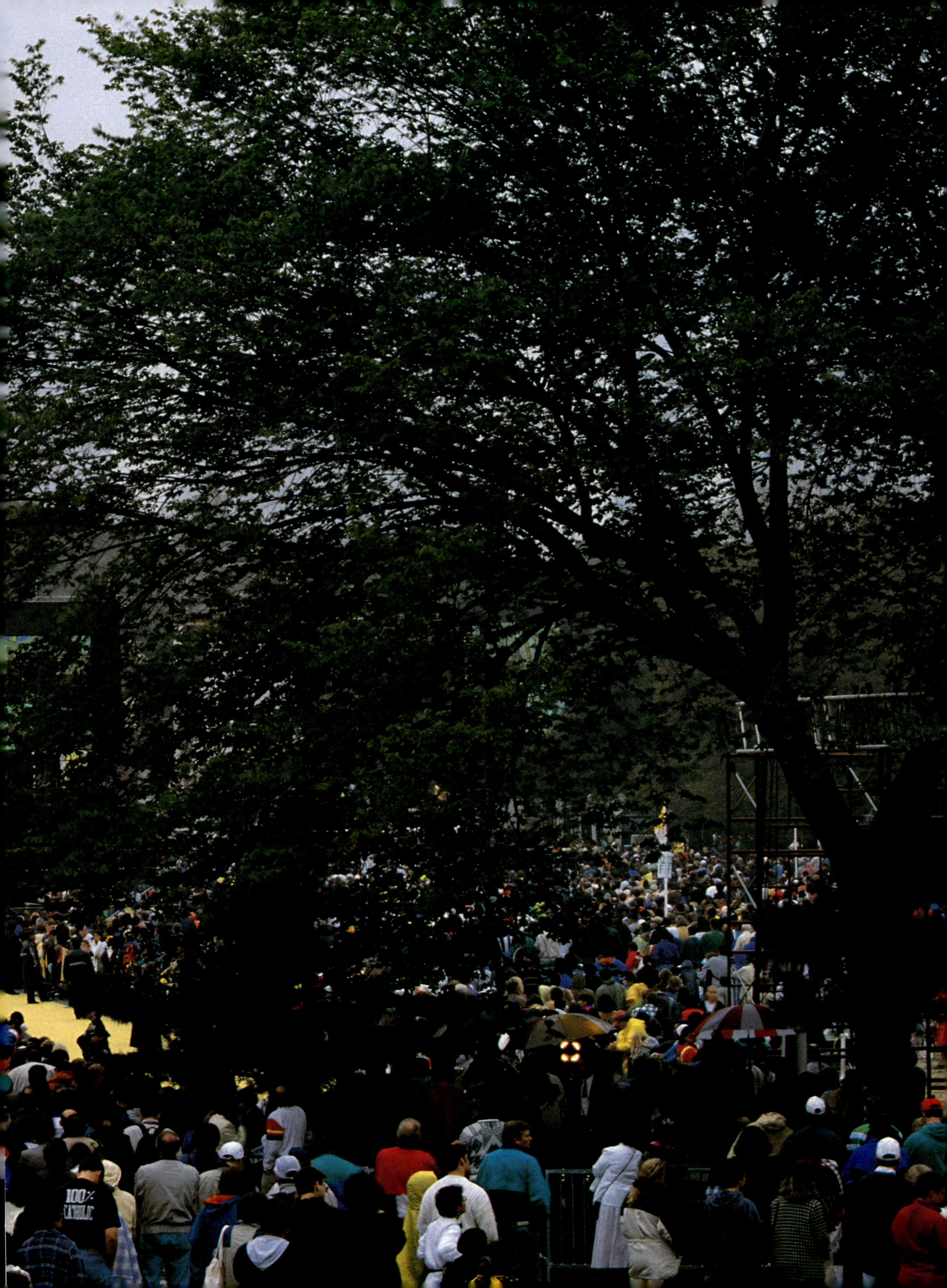
100%
CATHOLIC

NICARAGUA AND VENEZUELA

150 Caracas, Venezuela, 9th February, 1996. John Paul II prays before the statue of the Virgin Mary in the sanctuary of Coromoto. The Virgin appeared before the head of the Cospes tribe on 8th September 1652.

151 Managua, Nicaragua, 7th February, 1996. A glass case under a large red dome in the cathedral of Managua is the Chapel of the Blood of Christ. The cathedral is the most modern in the Americas.

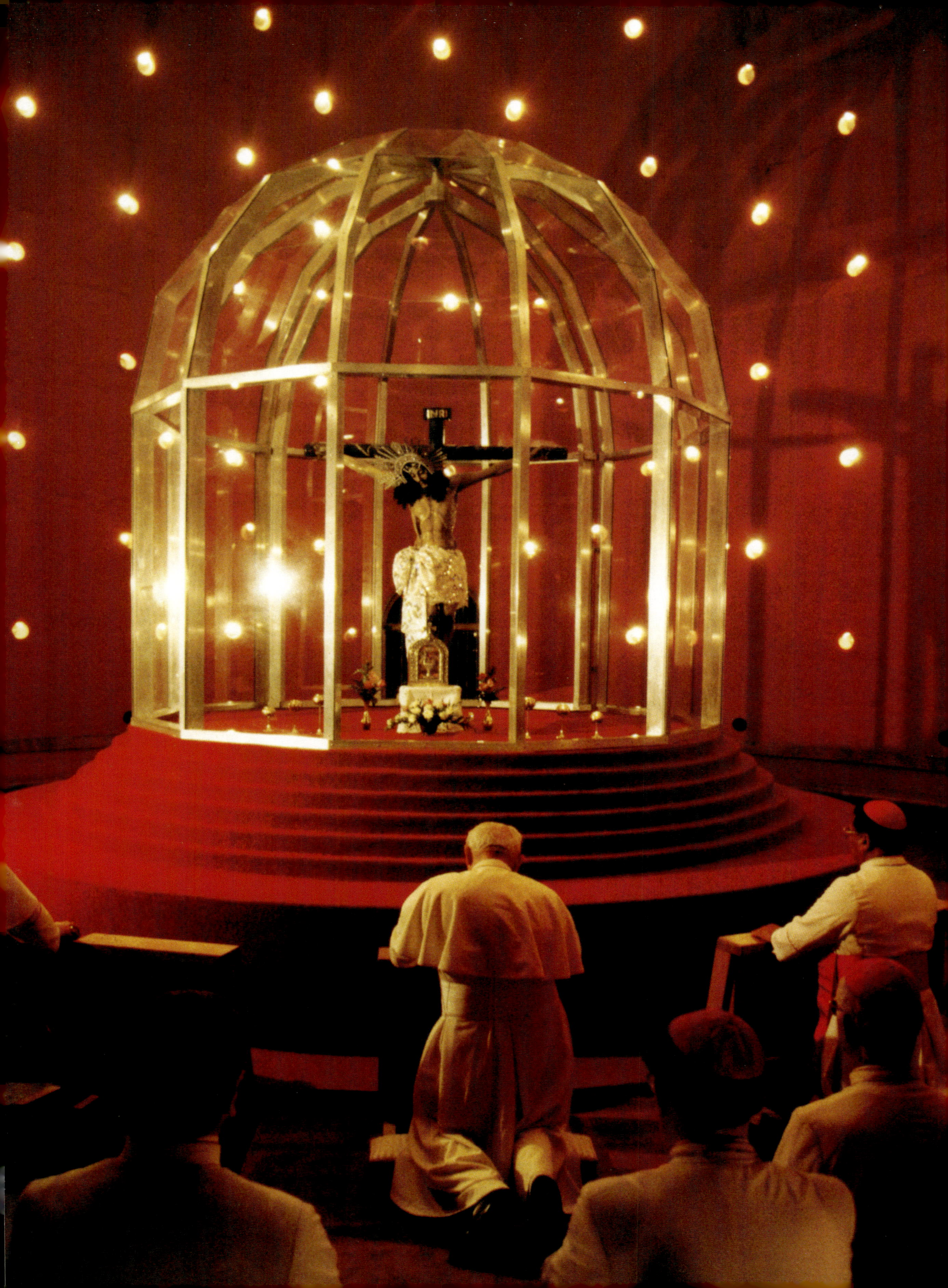

TUNISIA

152 Tunis, 14th April, 1996. The Pope met cultural and political representatives and religious figures in the presidential palace of Carthage.

152-153 Tunis, 14th April, 1996. The Pope reads his homily in the cathedral of Tunis. The patriarch Abraham can be seen above, blessing his descendants: Jews, Christians and Muslims.

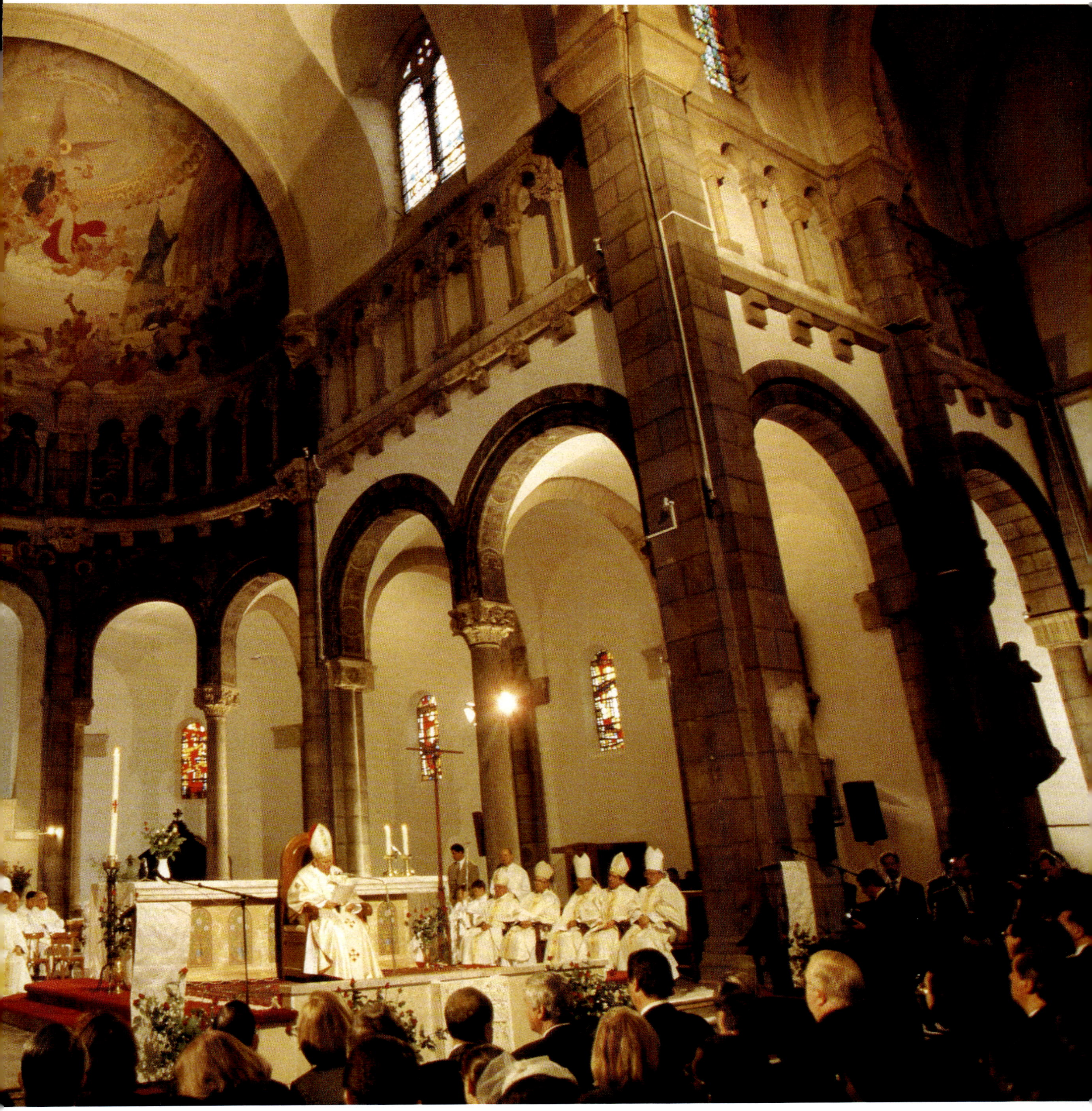

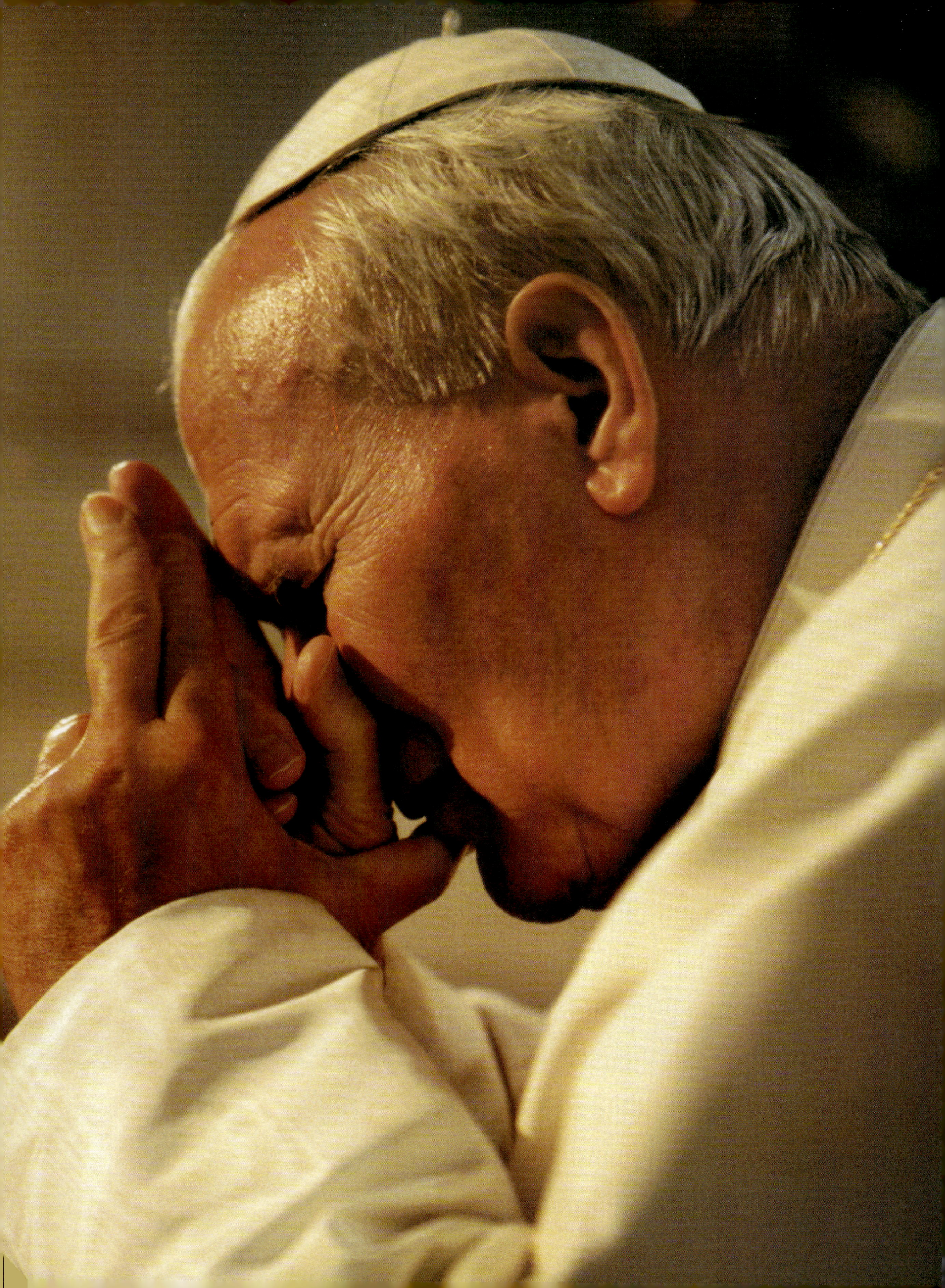

FRANCE

154 and 155 (top) *St. Laurent sur Sevre, 19th September, 1996. The Pope prays in the holy city of the Vendée, in the basilica dedicated to St. Lawrence the Martyr.*

155 (center) *Tours, 21st September, 1996. The Pope in the basilica of St. Martin, to meet the sick, the disabled, the poor and the elderly, in remembrance of St. Martin and following in his trail.*

155 (bottom) *S.te Anne d'Auray, 21st September, 1996. In the agricultural town of St. Anne d'Auray, in Brittany, the Pope surrounded by an enthusiastic, joyous crowd.*

156 Longchamp, 23rd August, 1997. Tens of thousands of young people from all over the world take part in the vigil with the Pope in the hippodrome of Longchamp for the World Day of Youth.

157 Paris, 21st August, 1997. The luminous sign shows the countdown to the new millennium. The Pope remembers human rights in Palais Chaillot.

J - 863
AVANT L'AN 2000

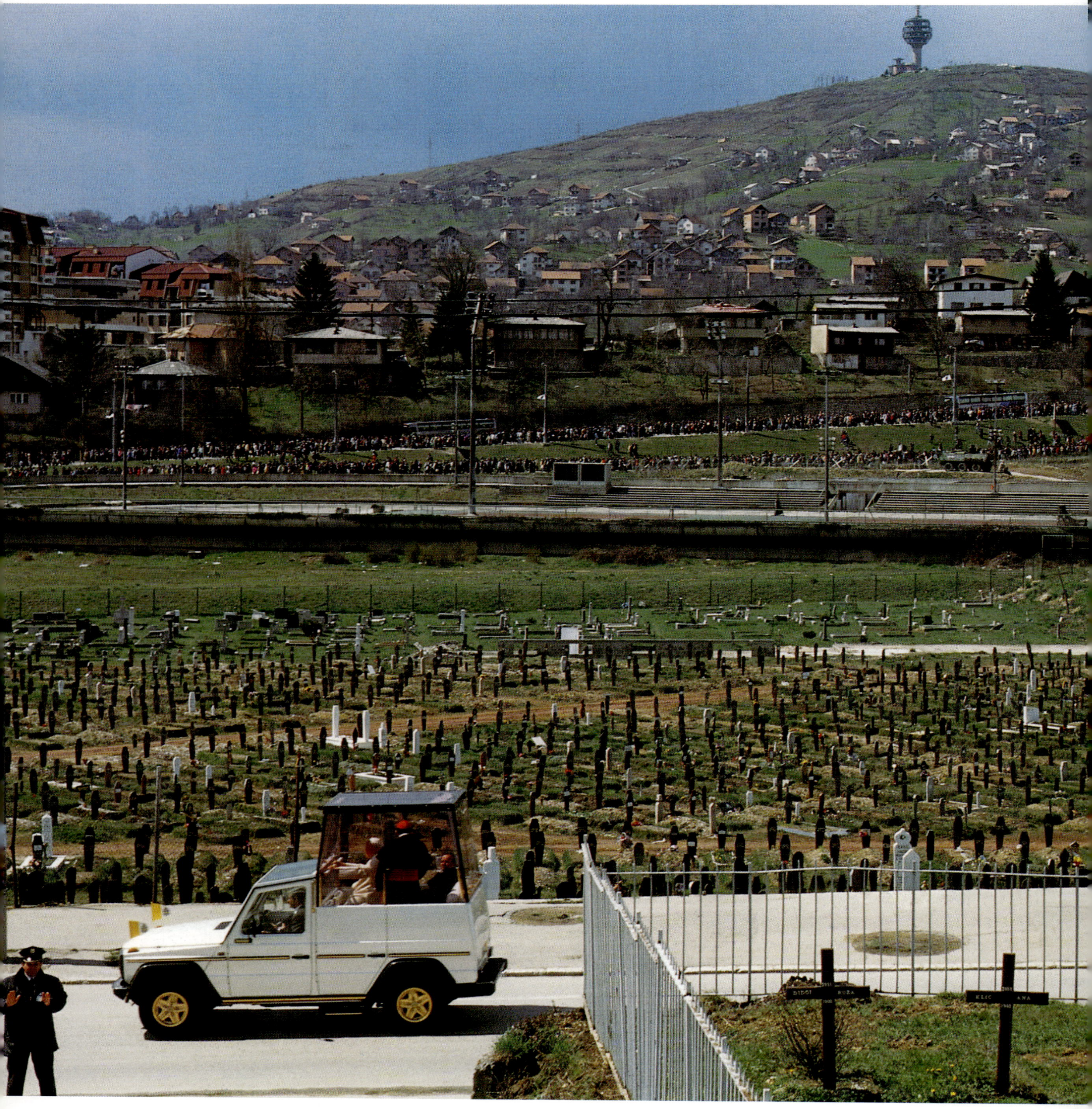
KLIC ANA

BOSNIA - HERZEGOVINA

158-159 *Sarajevo, 13rd April, 1997. The Popemobile leaves the Olympic Stadium after mass, and drives past the war graves.*

159 *Sarajevo, 13rd April, 1997. It is snowing in the stadium of Sarajevo, as John Paul II conducts mass. A canon shelters him with an umbrella.*

CUBA

160 Havana, Plaza de la Revolucion, 23rd January, 1998. Two opposing symbols meet in the square, site of the vast gatherings ordered by Fidel Castro and the biggest ever mass by Pope Wojtyla. The profile of the hero, Ernesto "Che" Guevara, and the traditional image of the Sacred Heart of Jesus, worshipped on the island.

161 Santiago de Cuba, January, 1998. The most famous photograph of the journey at the end of the century. Fidel Castro, who set his olive green uniform aside for the occasion, at the Pope's side.

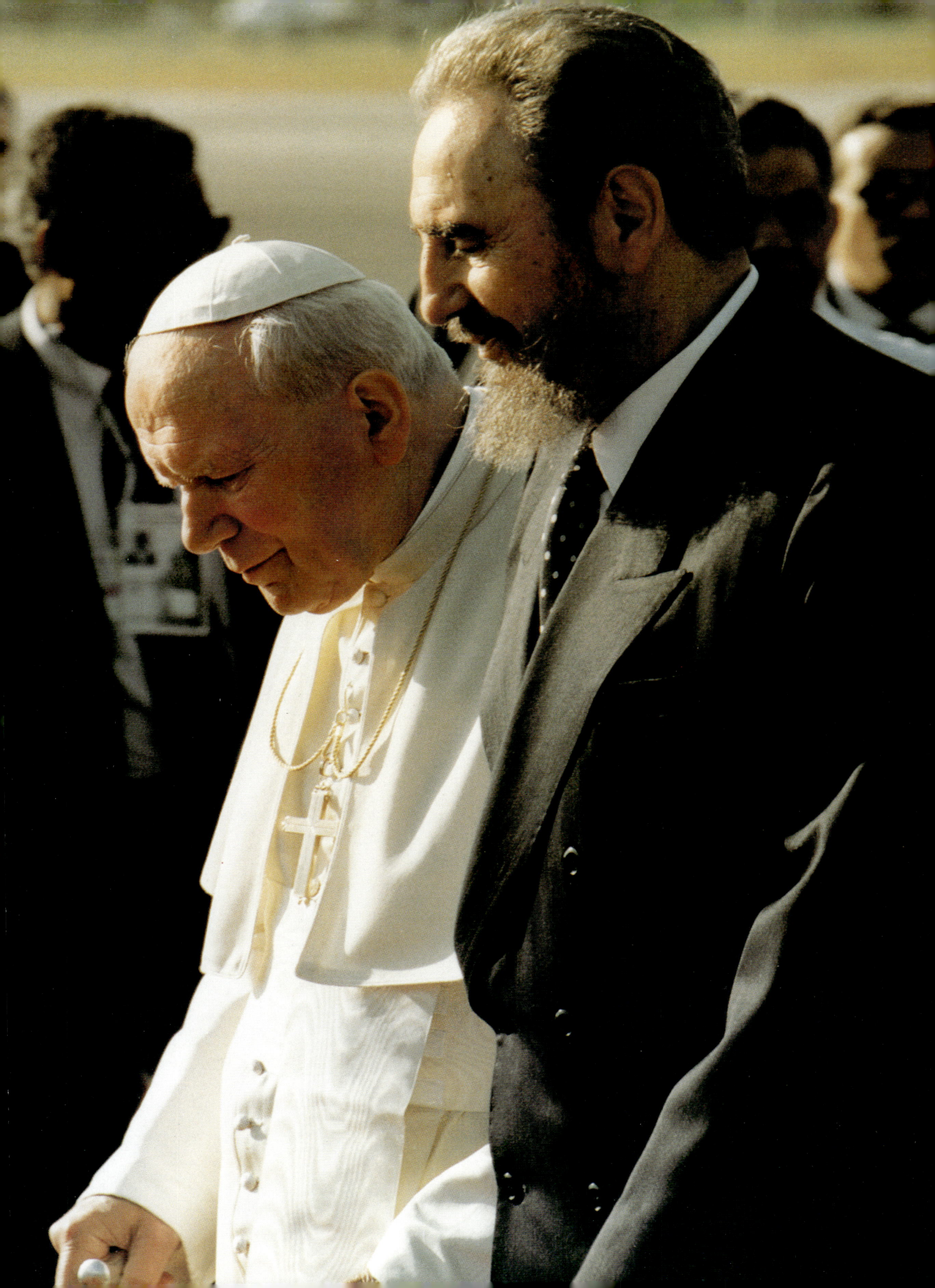

162 *Havana, 23rd January, 1998.
Fidel Castro shows the Pope the most precious
gift, a biography of Felix Varela, the Cuban
priest who fought to free the island from Spanish
rule in the 19th century. Only ten copies of the
book remain throughout the world.*

162-163 *Santiago de Cuba, 24th January, 1998.
An emotional audience listen to the Pope
as he asks for religious and civil liberty for the
people of Cuba.*

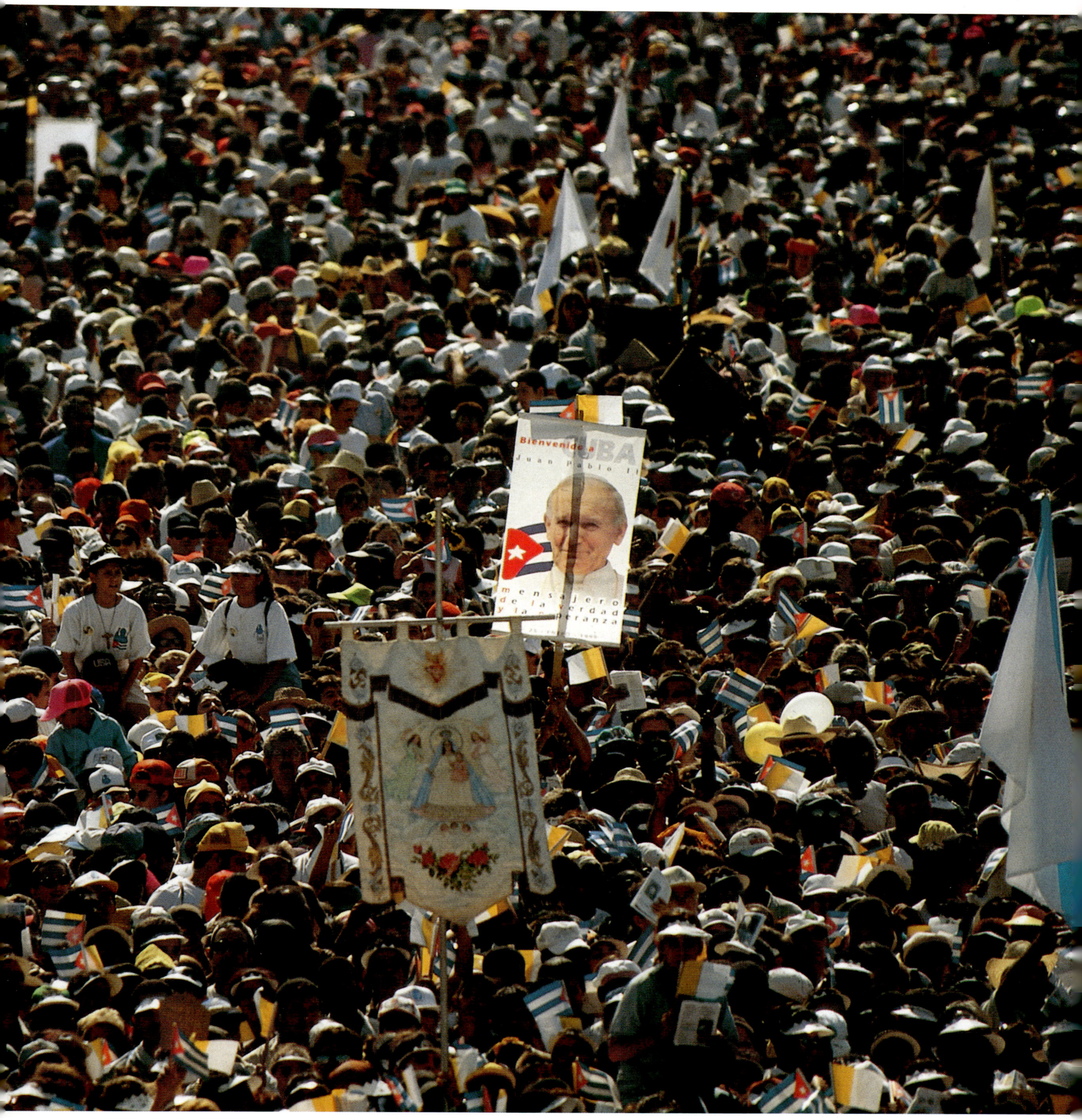
Juan Pablo II
mensajero
de la verdad

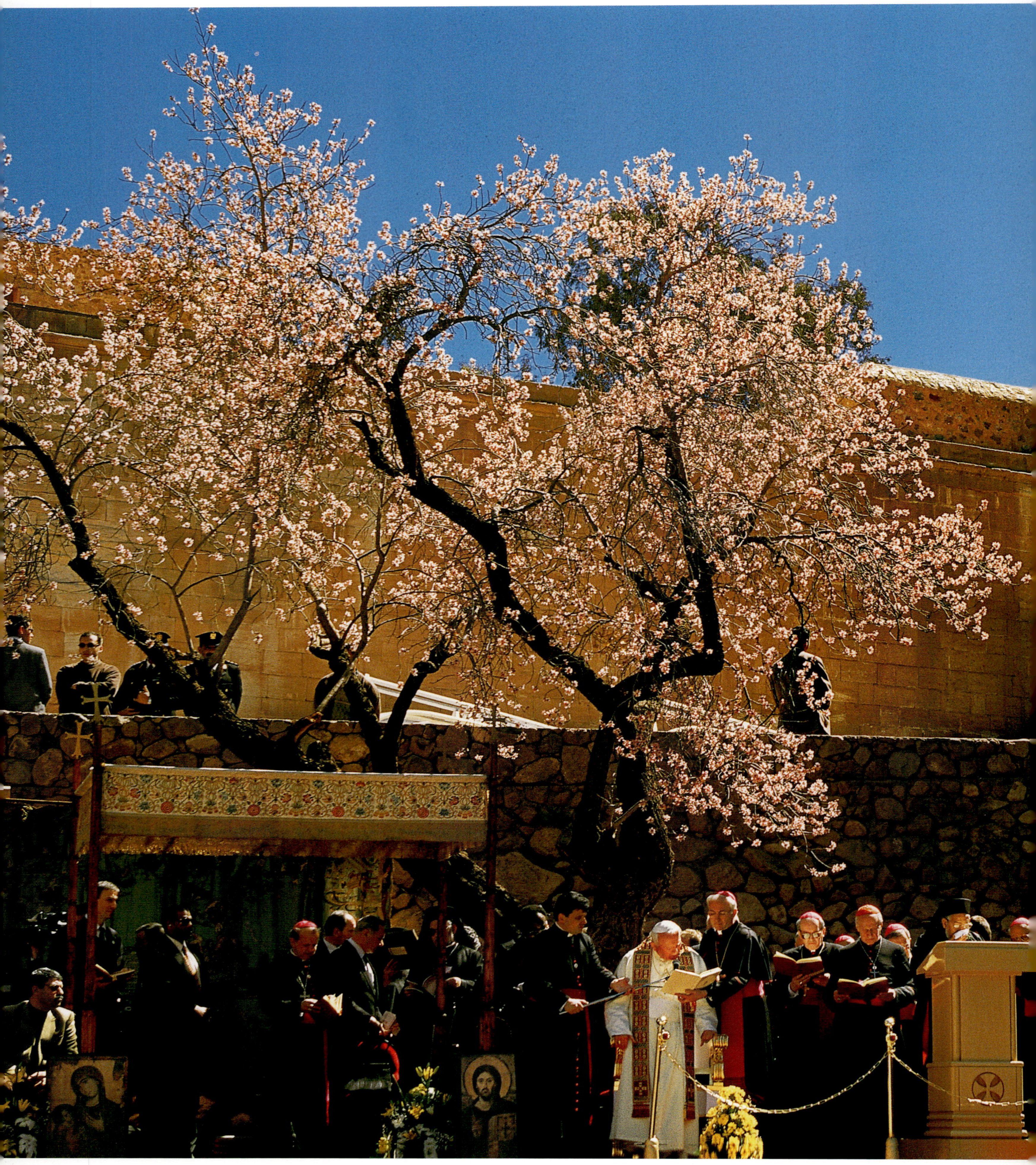

EGYPT

164-165 Santa Caterina, February 2000. The Pope recites a prayer with the hegumen Damianos, in the Garden of Olives in St. Catherine's monastery.

165 (top) St. Catherine's, February 2000. John Paul II is welcomed on his arrival by the Archbishop Damanios at St. Catherine's monastery.

165 (bottom) St. Catherine's, February 2000. The Pope greets the faithful who have gathered to meet him.

166-167 Madaba, 20 March 2000. On his arrival at the ancient monastery, the Pope embraces a child who has come to welcome him. The Moses memorial was built in the first half of the 4th century by Christians in the region of Madaba to commemorate the famous episode in the Bible (Deuteronomy 34).

167 (top) Amman, 20 March 2000. John Paul II is received at the "Queen Alia" international airport by the young ruler of Jordan, Abdallah II. This was the second visit of a Pope to the country; the first was by Paul VI in January 1964.

JORDAN

167 (bottom) *Madaba, 20 March 2000. The Pope looks over the Jordan Valley from the balcony.*

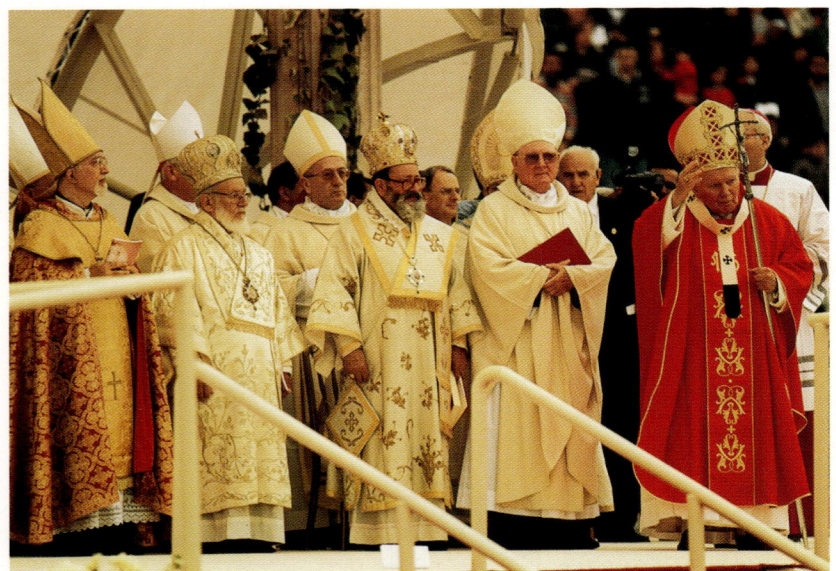

168 (top) *Amman, 21 March 2000. Mass is celebrated in Amman Stadium in Al-Hussein Sports City.*

168 (center) *Amman, 21 March 2000. John Paul II blesses the faithful.*

168 (bottom) *Amman, 21 March 2000. The Mass is the opportunity for the Pope to meet the Christian community of Jordan.*

169 *Amman, 21 March 2000. This was a moment of intense emotion for the Pope during the celebration of the Eucharist in Amman Stadium.*

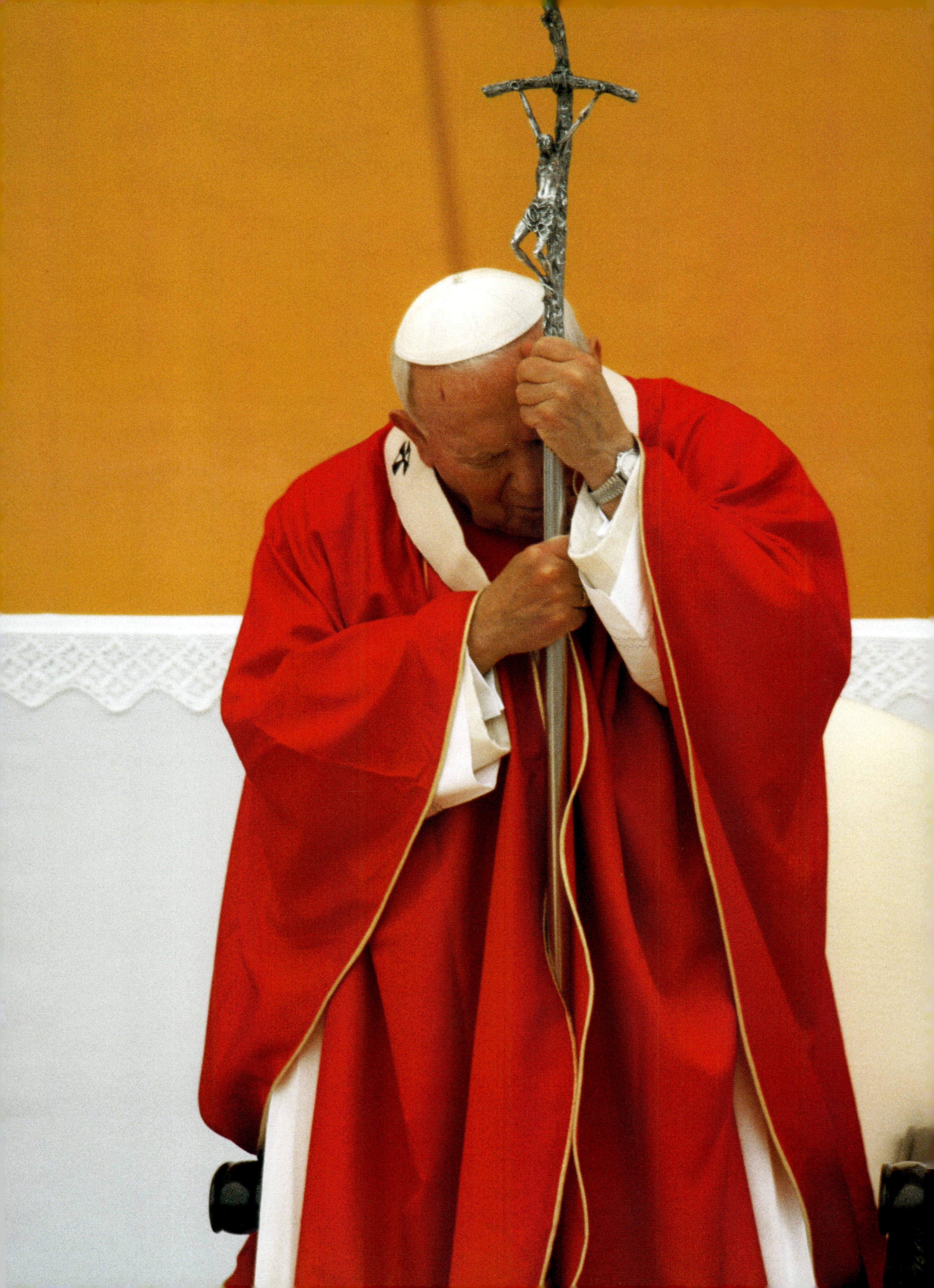

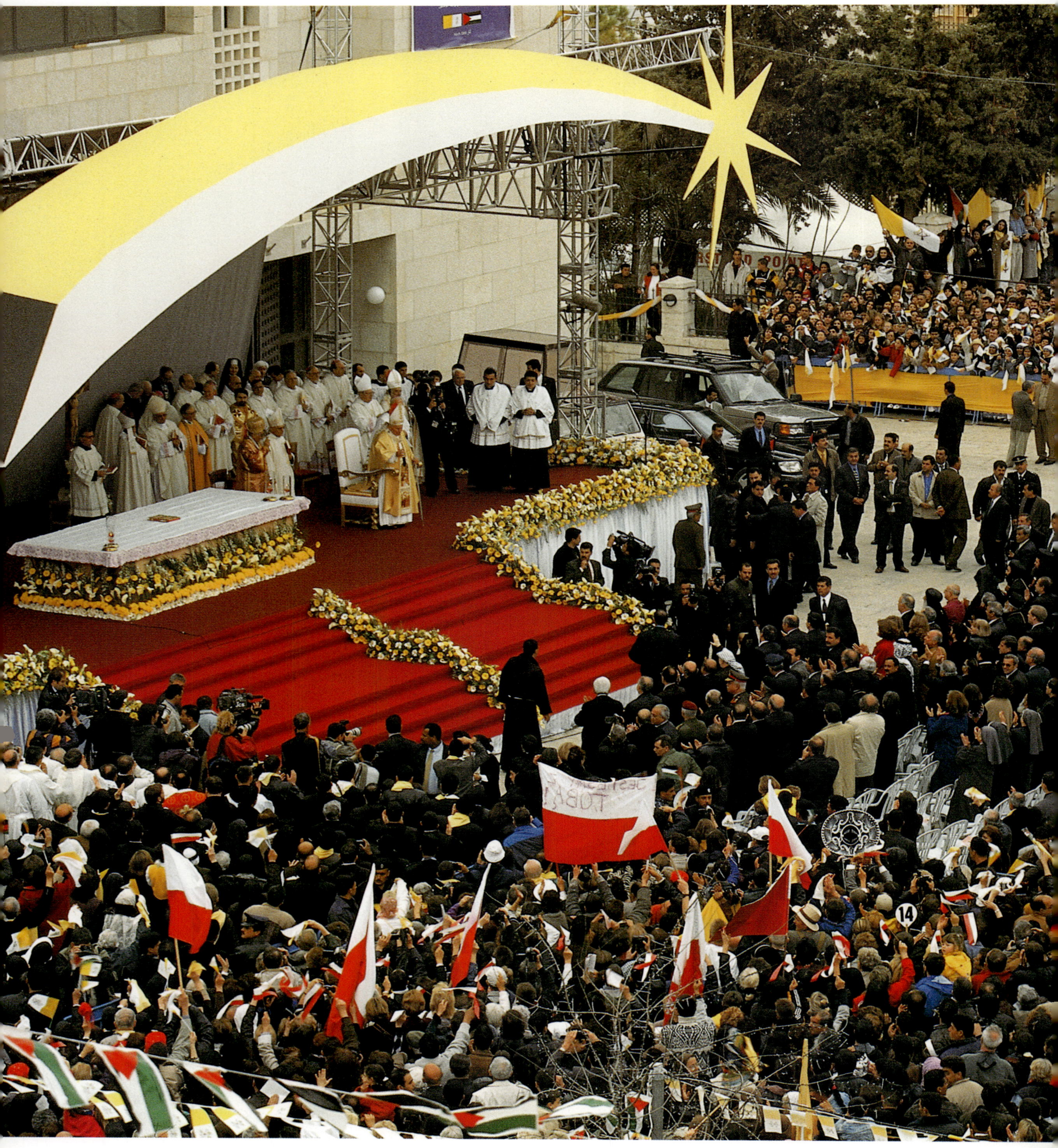

PALESTINE

170-171 *Bethlehem, 22 March 2000. The Pope officiates on the raised podium at the mass in front of the Church of the Nativity. Manger Square, the largest square in Bethlehem, is surrounded by the City Hall, an ancient mosque, and the Peace Building.*

171 *Bethlehem, 22 March 2000. Bad weather forced the organizers to improvise a ceremony in the Presidential Palace, where the Pope was welcomed by Yasser Arafat and his young wife.*

ISRAEL

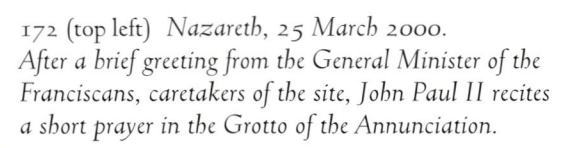

172 (top left) *Nazareth, 25 March 2000. After a brief greeting from the General Minister of the Franciscans, caretakers of the site, John Paul II recites a short prayer in the Grotto of the Annunciation.*

172 (right) *Nazareth, 25 March 2000. The Pope celebrates Mass in the Basilica of the Annunciation. The Franciscan church built in 1730 incorporates the grotto-house of the Holy Family in a crypt below the high altar. The large central mosaic is the work of artist Salvatore Fiume.*

172 (bottom left) *Korazim, 24 March 2000. The Mass, held in front of the Domus Galilaeae on the hill where the Sermon on the Mount was given, was dedicated to children.*

173 *Korazim, 24 March 2000. John Paul II looks towards the 100,000 youths who have come from all over the Holy Land and nearby countries. The ceremony was held above Tangha in front of Lake Tiberias where, according to the Bible, the feeding of the five thousand took place.*

AMATE I VOSTRI NEMICI VENGO PRESTO

טרזינשטט · THERESIENSTADT

174 *Jerusalem, 23 March 2000. Visiting the mausoleum of Yad Veshem, the monument to the memory of the Holocaust, the Pope is greeted at the entrance to the Hall of Remembrance by Prime Minister Ehud Barak and the two Grand Rabbis of Israel, Meir Lau and Mordechai Bakshi-Doron.*

175 (left) *Jerusalem, 23 March 2000. John Paul II is overcome by a moment of great emotion.*

175 (right) *Jerusalem 23 March 2000. After laying a crown of flowers on the tomb containing the ashes of victims of many concentration camps, the Pope reads his speech of solidarity with the Jewish people.*

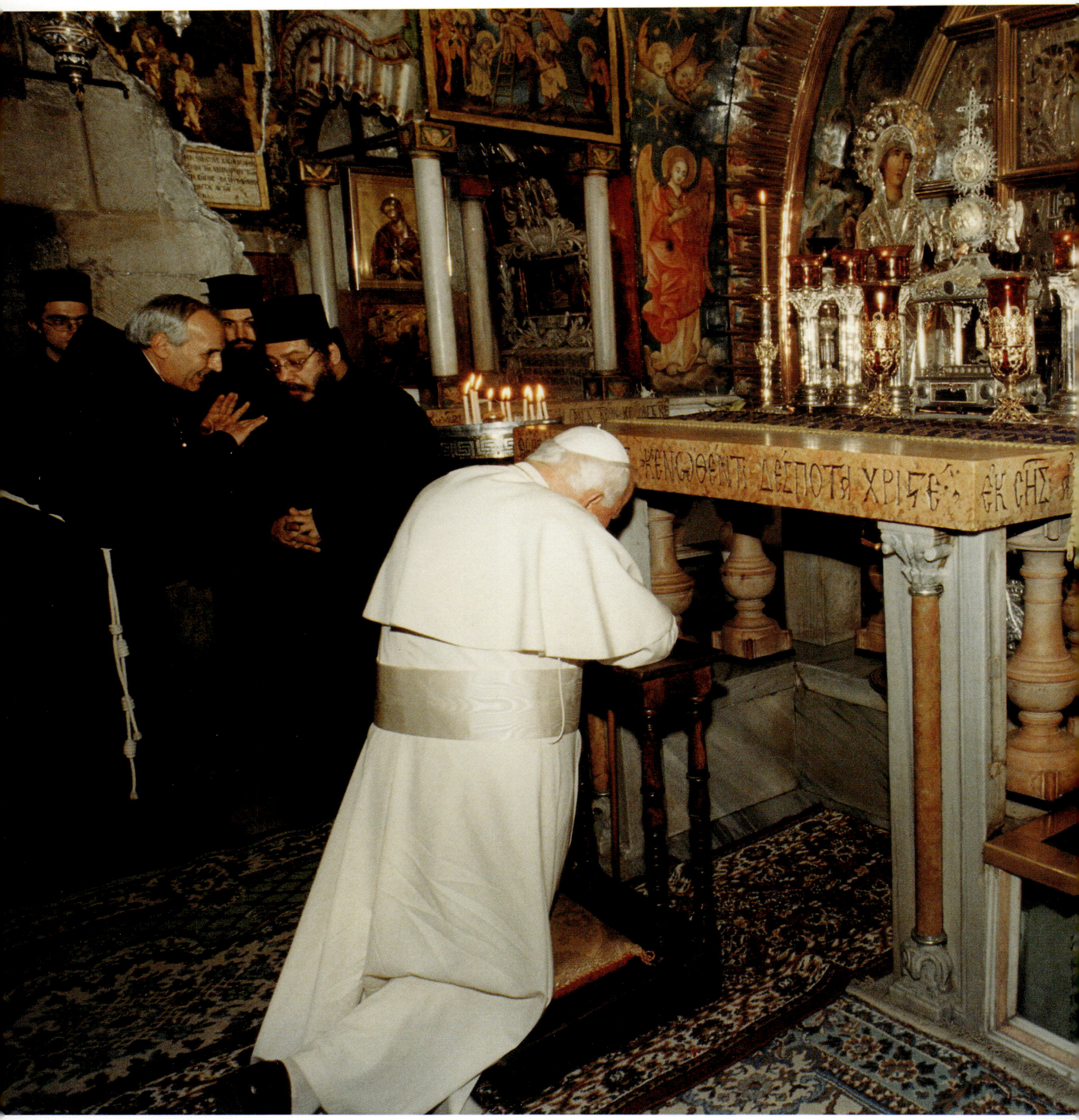

176-177 and 177 Jerusalem, 26 March 2000.
The Pope prays in the Holy Sepulchre, where according to tradition the crucifixion, the burial, and the resurrection of Christ took place.
"They took the body of Jesus and wrapped it in linen cloths with spices as was the custom amongst the Jews" (John 19:38).

178 and 178-179 *Jerusalem, 26th March 2000. John Paul II stops in an attitude of concentration before the Western Wall, after symbolically inserting a note in the space between two blocks of stone, containing the words of the Mea culpa he read out in St. Peter's on 21st March.*

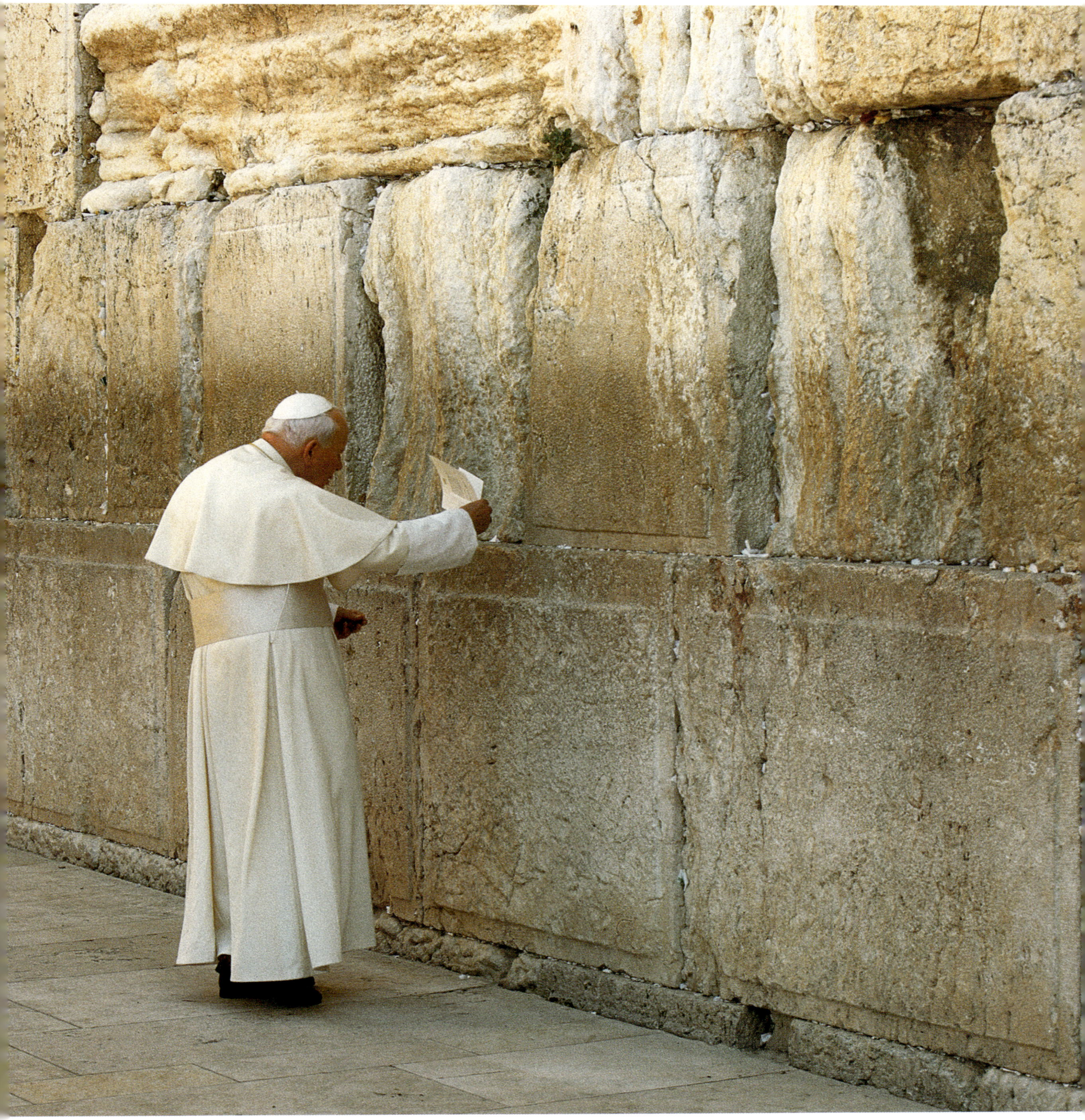

PORTUGAL

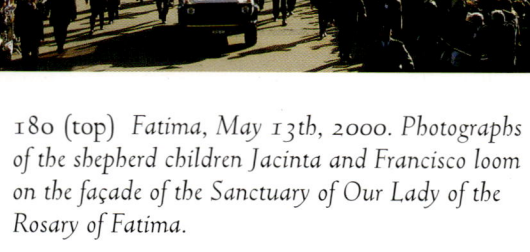

180 (top) Fatima, May 13th, 2000. Photographs of the shepherd children Jacinta and Francisco loom on the façade of the Sanctuary of Our Lady of the Rosary of Fatima.

180 (bottom) *Fatima, May 13th, 2000. The papal limousine moves between two wings of the crowd in the esplanade in front of the Sanctuary of Our Lady of the Rosary.*

180-181 *Fatima, May 13th 2000. The faithful, gathered for the beatification ceremony of Jacinta and Francisco Marto, give John Paul II an extraordinary welcome.*

182-183 Quneitra, Syria, May 7th, 2001. John Paul II receives a kiss from a little girl, a member of the Greek Orthodox Church, during the Prayers for Peace.

SYRIA, GREECE AND MALTA

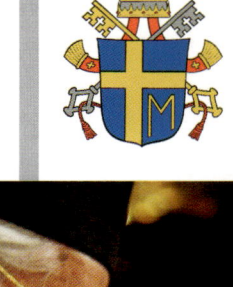

183 (top) *Damascus, Syria, May 7th, 2001. Pope John Paul II meets the Patriarch Gregory III Laham: an historic embrace during the meeting with young people in the Greek Orthodox cathedral.*

183 (bottom) *Damascus, Syria, May 7th, 2001. The papal limousine has difficulty moving through the narrow channel left open by the sea of young faithful.*

UKRAINE, KAZAKHSTAN AND ARMENIA

184 (top) Astana, Kazakhstan, September 22nd, 2001. John Paul II meets some illustrious figures from the worlds of culture, the arts and science in the auditorium of the Congress Hall in the capital.

184 (bottom) Astana, Kazakhstan, September 22nd, 2001. The President of the Republic of Kazakhstan, M. Nursultan Abishevich Nazarbayev and his family receive the Pontiff in the Presidential Palace.

184-185 *Lviv, Ukraine, June 27th, 2001.*
Cardinal Lubomyr Husar kisses John Paul II's hand
during a beatification liturgy in the Byzantine Rite.

186-187 Baku, May 22nd, 2002. A gust of wind knocks John Paul II's skull cap off: this is one of the more informal moments that marked the meeting with President M. Heidar Aliev.

AZERBAIJAN

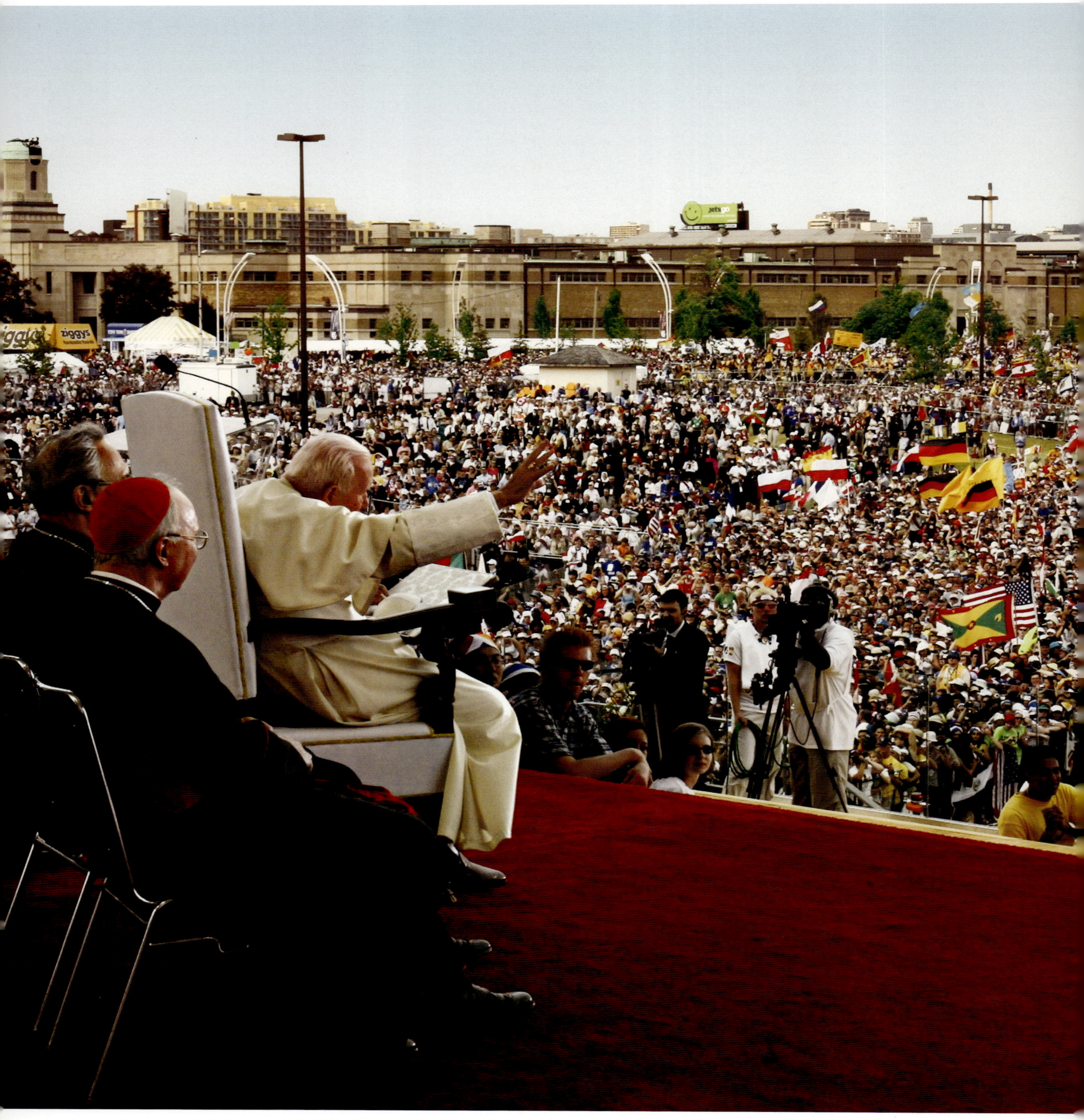
ziggys
jetsgo

CANADA

188-189 *Toronto, July 2002. A vast audience made up of faithful from the world over takes part in the Mass celebrated in Exhibition Place, for the 17th World Youth Day at Downsview Park.*

MEXICO

190 Mexico City, July 31st, 2002. John Paul II's armored limousine moves through the crowds toward the new Basilica of Nuestra Señora de Guadalupe (left of picture), opposite the old basilica built in the Mexican Baroque style.

190-191 and 192-193 Mexico City, July 31st, 2002. John Paul II celebrates the canonization of Juan Diego Cuauhtlatoatzin in the Basilica Nuestra Señora de Guadalupe. Indigenous people in traditional dress take part in the ceremony, in the ultra-modern building of the basilica, which can contain thousands of people.

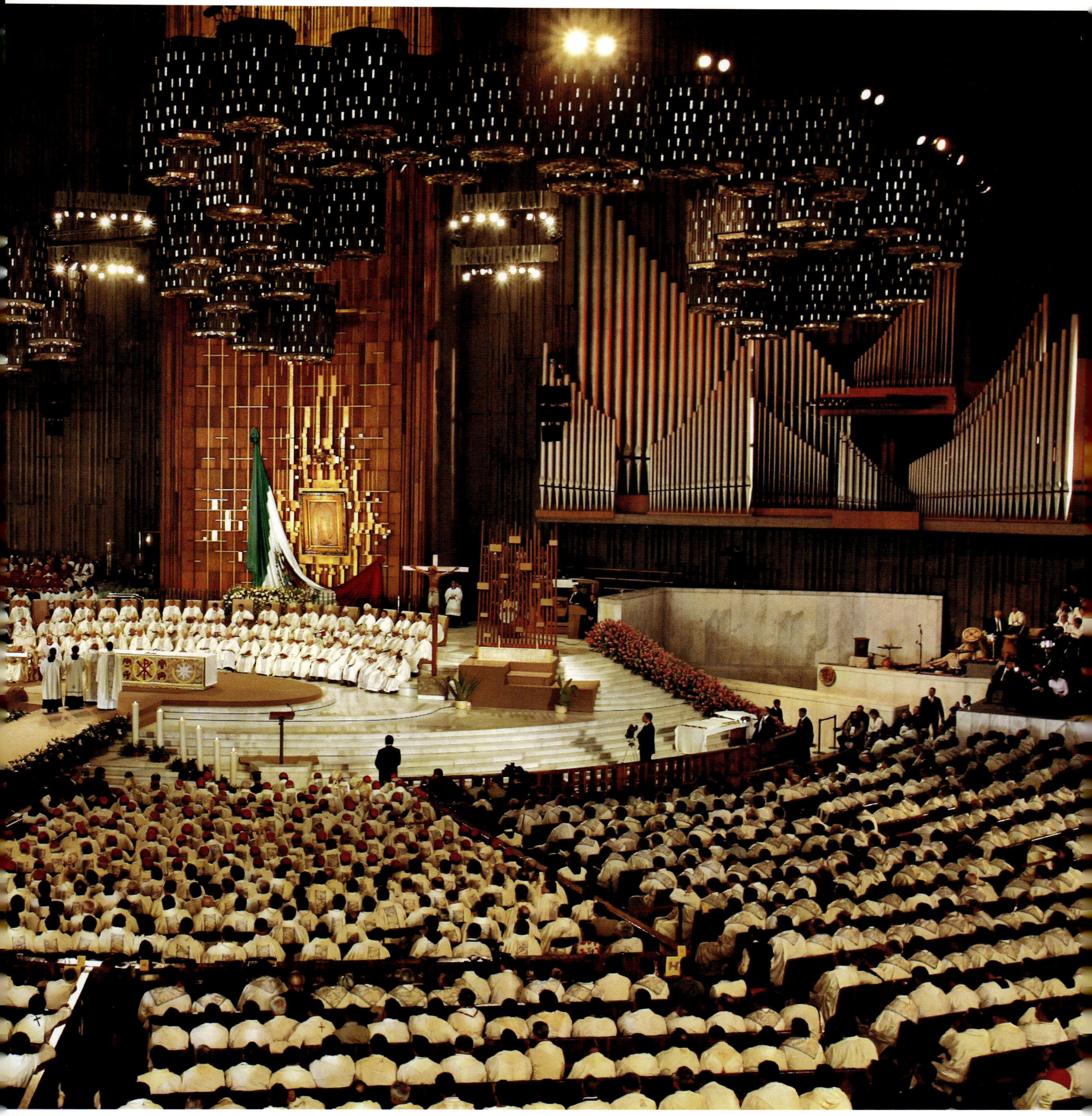

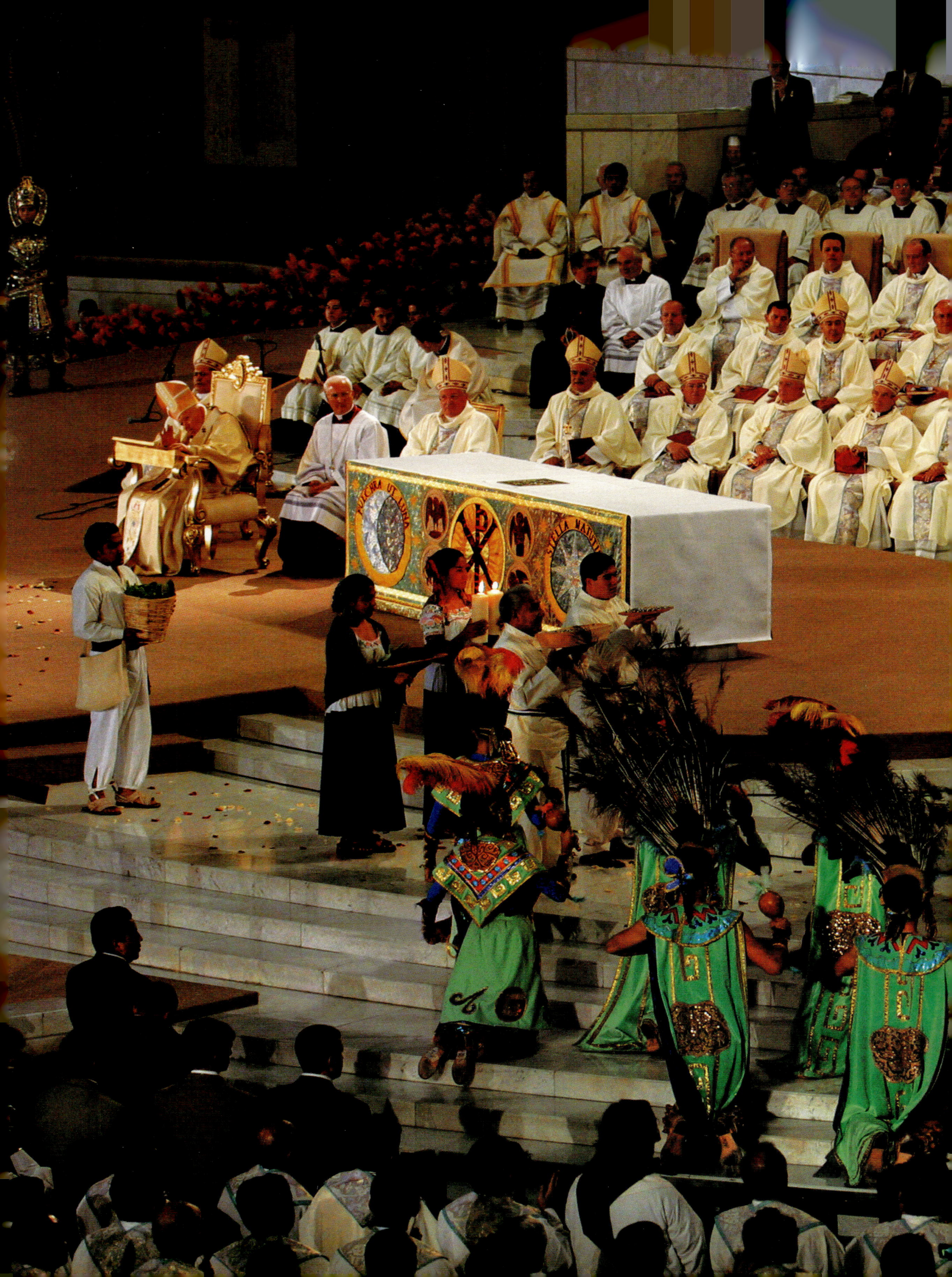
PULCHRA UT LUNA

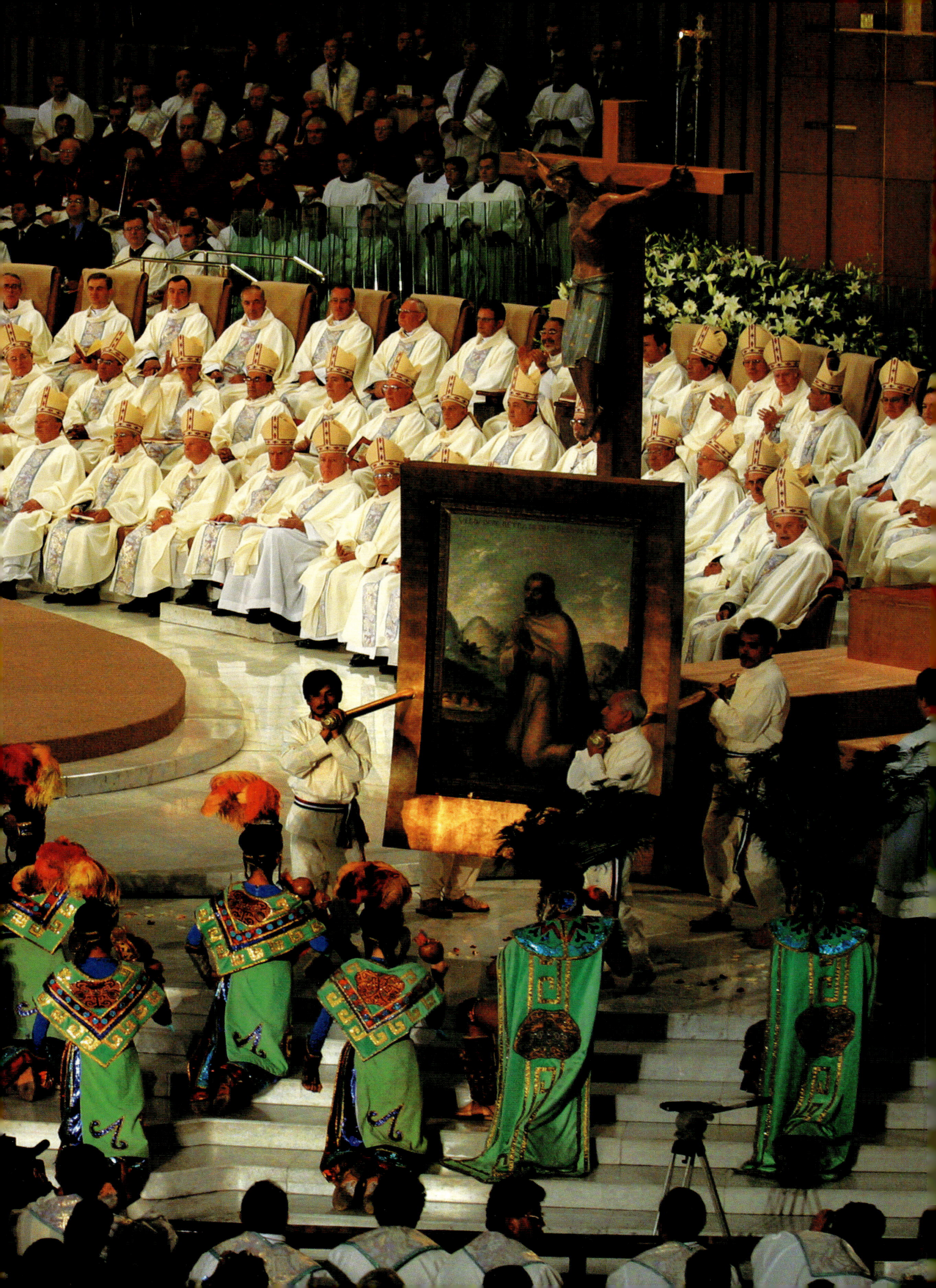

GUATEMALA

194 *Guatemala City, July 2002. In a telling and intense image, Pope John Paul II is captured in a moment of reflection upon arrival at La Aurora international airport.*

194-195 *Guatemala City, July 2002. Jean Paul II meets a mother with her child during the canonization ceremony of Hermano Pedro de San José, celebrated at the Hippodrome in Guatemala City.*

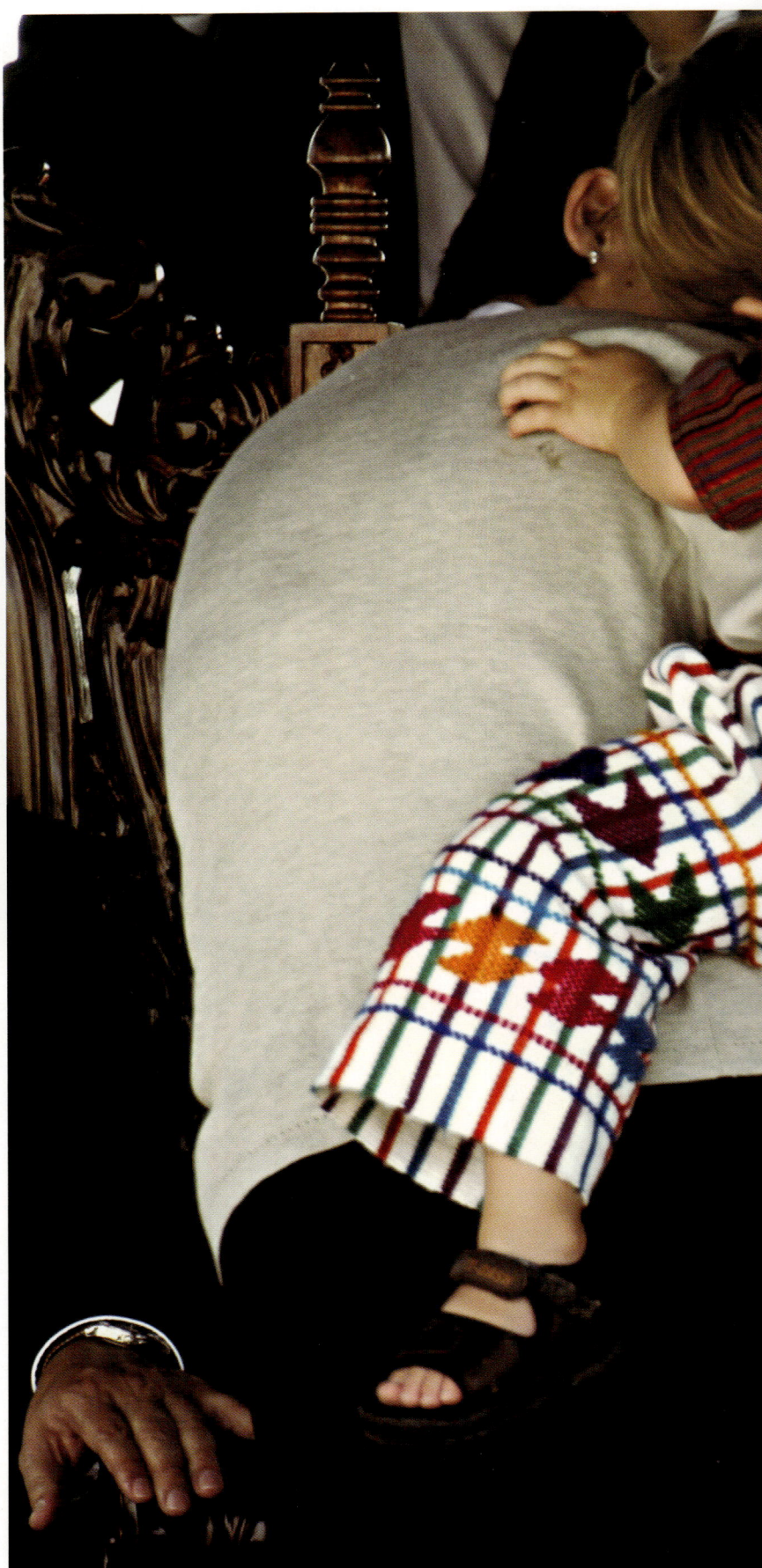

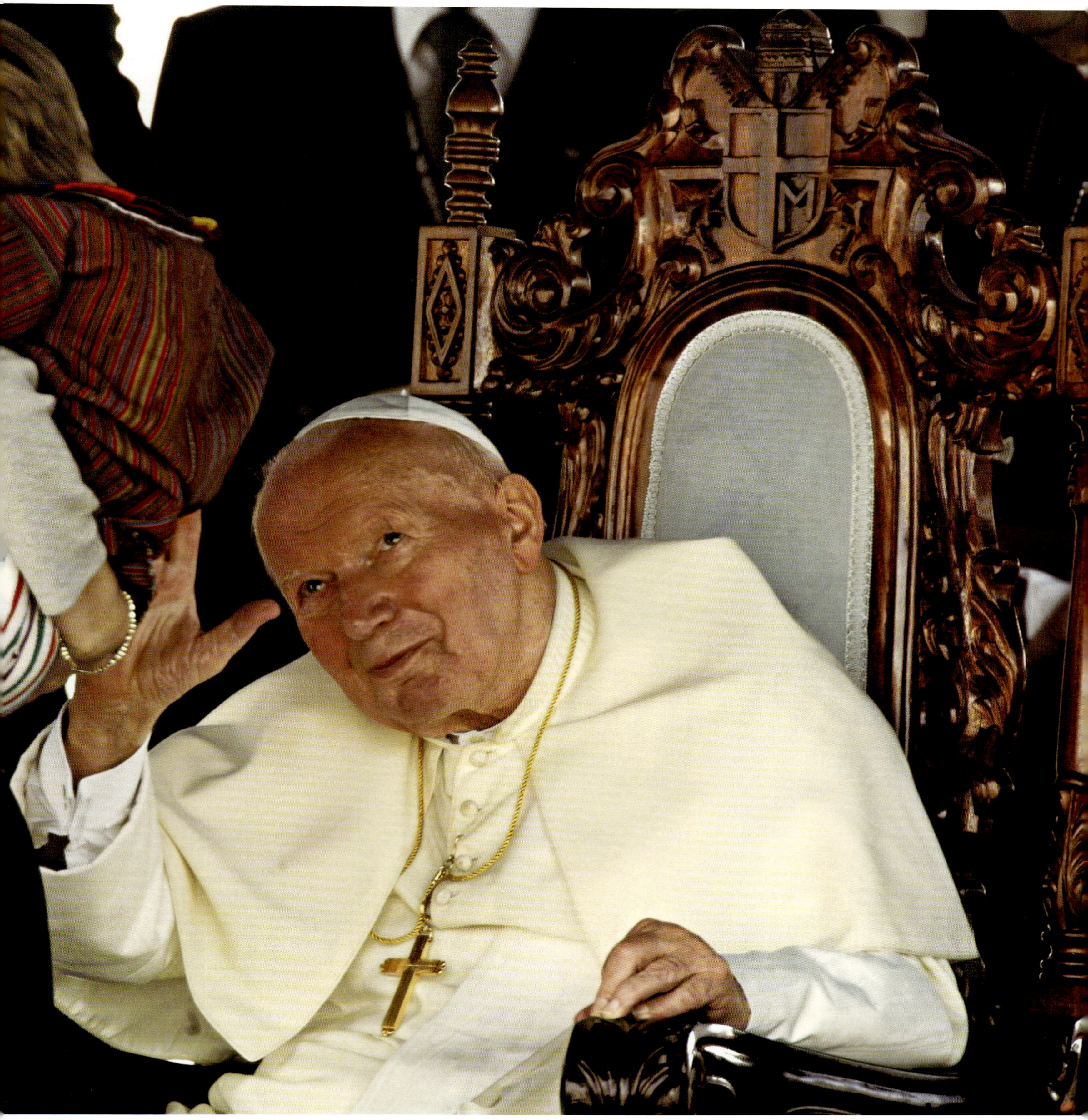

196-197 *Kraków, August 2002. John Paul II celebrates Holy Mass during the ceremony of the Dedication of the Sanctuary of Divine Mercy in Kraków-Lagiewniki.*

POLAND

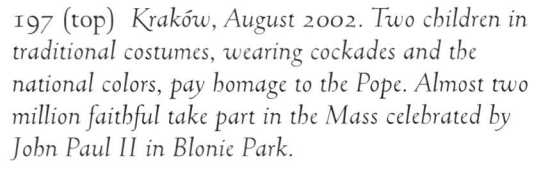

197 (top) *Kraków, August 2002. Two children in traditional costumes, wearing cockades and the national colors, pay homage to the Pope. Almost two million faithful take part in the Mass celebrated by John Paul II in Blonie Park.*

197 (bottom) *Kraków, August 2002. The Pope visits the tomb of his parents, Karol Wojtyla and Emilia Kaczorowska, in the cemetery at Rakowice.*

SWITZERLAND

198 Berne, June 5th, 2004. With the Swiss Guard before him, John Paul II greets the young Swiss Catholics who have gathered in the Ice Palace at Bea Bern Expo.

198-199 Berne, June 5th, 2004. John Paul receives a round of applause from those taking part in the great Swiss gathering. By his side is Cardinal Angelo Sodano, the Secretary of State of the Holy See.

199

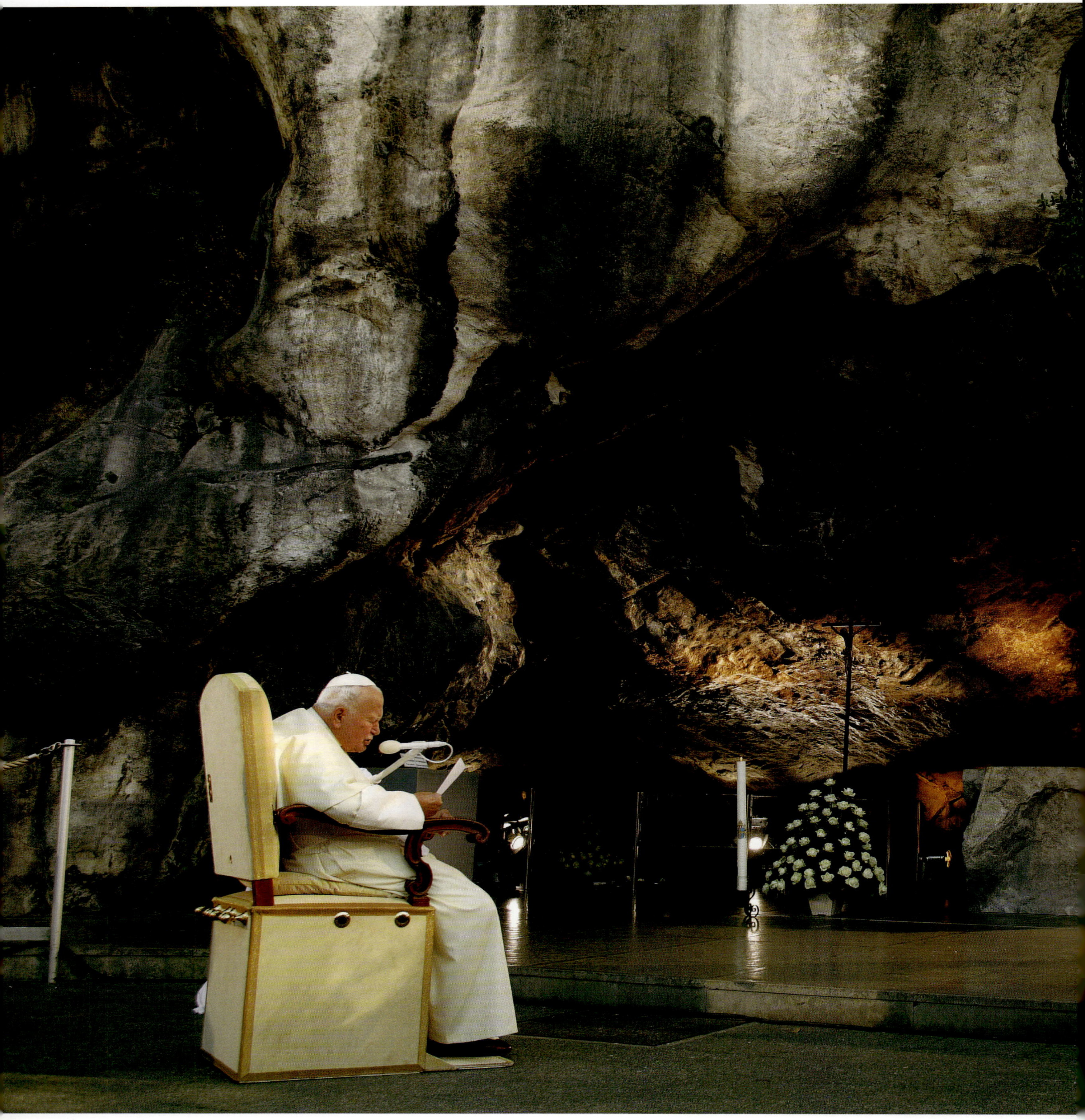

FRANCE

200-201 *Lourdes, August 14th, 2004. John Paul speaks to the sick, facing the Grotto of Apparitions in Massabielle.*

201 (top) *Lourdes, August 14th, 2004. On the papal vehicle, John Paul II reaches the Chapelle de Notre-Dame de Lourdes to watch the procession of the Holy Rosary.*

201 (bottom) *Lourdes, August 14th, 2004. During the procession of the Holy Rosary, the Pope blesses some of the sick that are present.*

The Last Farewell

The crisis began on the evening of 1 February 2005. We were told that it all began with a simple bout of flu, which is a very common illness but can have drastic consequences for elderly people suffering from other illnesses, as John Paul II did. The infection actually began on Saturday, January 29th; a high fever, mucus, some difficulty in speaking, which became obvious during the Angelus on Sunday, January 30th. His voice was rasping, almost incomprehensible. The Pope's "family" immediately became alarmed. Indeed, one of the dangers of Parkinson's disease, apart from the falls, is the blockage of the muscles that allow swallowing and breathing. On the Monday afternoon, the respiratory problems began; an oxygen mask provided some relief, but only partially. This was just the beginning of an ordeal that was to last for two months. The difficulties returned on the Tuesday afternoon, before dinner. It was recommended that the Pope be admitted to hospital, and initially he was somewhat resistant to this idea. Later, just after dinner, he had another attack; the Gemelli Hospital was alerted, and a specialist quickly arrived at the Vatican. Once he had examined the Pope, he also recommended that he should be admitted to hospital. This took place – not without some further resistance on the Pope's part – at about 10.40pm. "Ten minutes later and it would have been too late", an anonymous spokesman later said.

Less than two weeks later, John Paul II left the Gemelli Hospital. He went on a sort of triumphal cavalcade home on the Popemobile across Rome to the Vatican, almost as though he wanted to prove, faced with rumours of resignation, that John Paul II was still Pope.

This was a brief interlude of apparent calm; on February 23rd, in a video conference from his study,

202-203 Baku, Azerbaijan, May 2002 –
Pope John Paul II, who has just landed at Baku
International airport, looks outside through the
bullet-proof glass of the car he is traveling in.

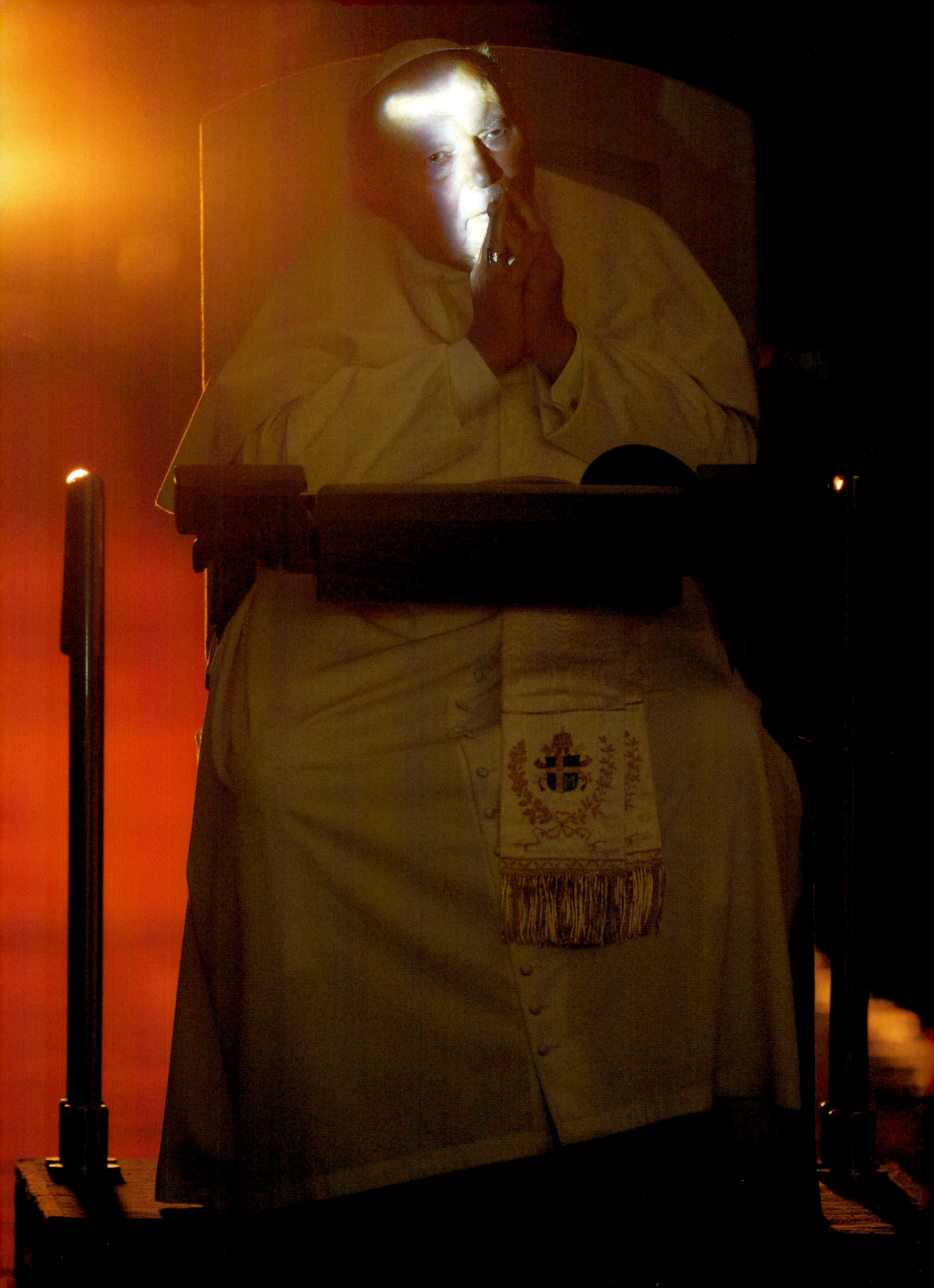

John Paul II greeted the crowds of faithful who had gathered in the Paul VI room. But this interlude was all too short; and indeed, on February 24th there was a new emergency, followed by urgent admission to the Gemelli Hospital. It was morning, and after a quick consultation it was decided that a tracheotomy should be carried out: the insertion of a cannula into the throat, to help the Pope breathe, and to draw the mucus out of his lungs. "What have they done to me!", the Pontiff later wrote on his pad. Adding, "In any case, I'm still Totus Tuus," ("entirely yours," referring to his special veneration of the Virgin Mary). The second sentence that the Pope wrote was "Where is Wanda?", referring to Wanda Poltawska, the professor from Kraków who he had been friends with for a great many years, since right after the war. In fact, Wanda then spent almost every day at the hospital, reading in Polish to the Pope, who could no longer speak. However, after the tracheotomy things seemed to be improving: the Pope practised breathing and speaking with the cannula, and did so well that those who went to visit him said that he was able to express himself. Confirmation of this came on March 13th, when, during the recitation of the Angelus from the window of the tenth floor of the Gemelli Hospital, John Paul II made his voice heard once again: "Dear brothers and sisters, thank you for your visit," he said in Italian. And then immediately in Polish, "My regards to Wadowice." Finally, addressing the four hundred priests from a religious movement who were gathered in the square, "I greet the Legionnaires of Christ. I hope that all of you have a good Sunday." Wadowice is his town of birth, which he would also remember in his testament as "the city of my youth." The information filtering through from the hospital was definitely optimistic; it was said that John Paul II spent many hours a day out of bed, that he was receiving his collaborators, that he was even examining the dossiers that the Under-Secretary of State, Archbishop Sandri, brought to him. In brief, it seemed that the Pope was as active as ever.

And so he returned to the Vatican, where in his private chapel he followed the "Via Crucis," the meditations on which were written by Cardinal Ratzinger and paint a worrying picture of the Church as a boat tossed on the waves. We only saw Pope Wojtyla from behind as he embraced a crucifix, at the last station. On Sunday came the "Urbi et Orbi" message. Once again, Monsignor Sandri was the "voice" of Wojtyla. The Pope gave his blessing but was unable to speak. Just as he was unable to speak the following Wednesday, when he appeared for the last time at the study window; he nodded to the secretary Dom Mietek to bring the microphone closer, but no sound would come out of his throat, just a kind of rasping. John Paul II made a dejected gesture. The window closed. And it was not to open again. The Vatican announced that Pope John Paul was being fed through a "nasogastric" tube. Then, on Thursday, March 31st, his temperature rose suddenly; the lights in the papal apartments stayed on into the night, while doctors fought against a urinary infection. The situation seemed to stabilize, but the Pope's body was no longer able to react. His blood pressure fell. And Joaquin Navarro-Valls, the papal spokesman, unable to hide his emotion, announced gradually more serious information. John Paul was offered the option of going to the Gemelli Hospital, and he asked, "Is it necessary?" The doctors said no, and so he chose to stay at home and die there. On Saturday evening, soon after having heard the Mass for Divine Mercy, Pope John Paul II quietly passed away. It was 9.37pm on April 2nd, 2005. Karol Wojtyla wanted to finish as he had lived, a man of courage, praying, with his head held high.

204 *Vatican, November 2004 – Pope John Paul II attending the concert that the Russian army performed in the Sala Nervi to celebrate the 26th anniversary of his papal election.*

206-207 Rome, March 6th, 2005 – The Pope blesses the pilgrims who have gathered beneath the windows of the Gemelli Hospital for the Sunday Angelus prayer.

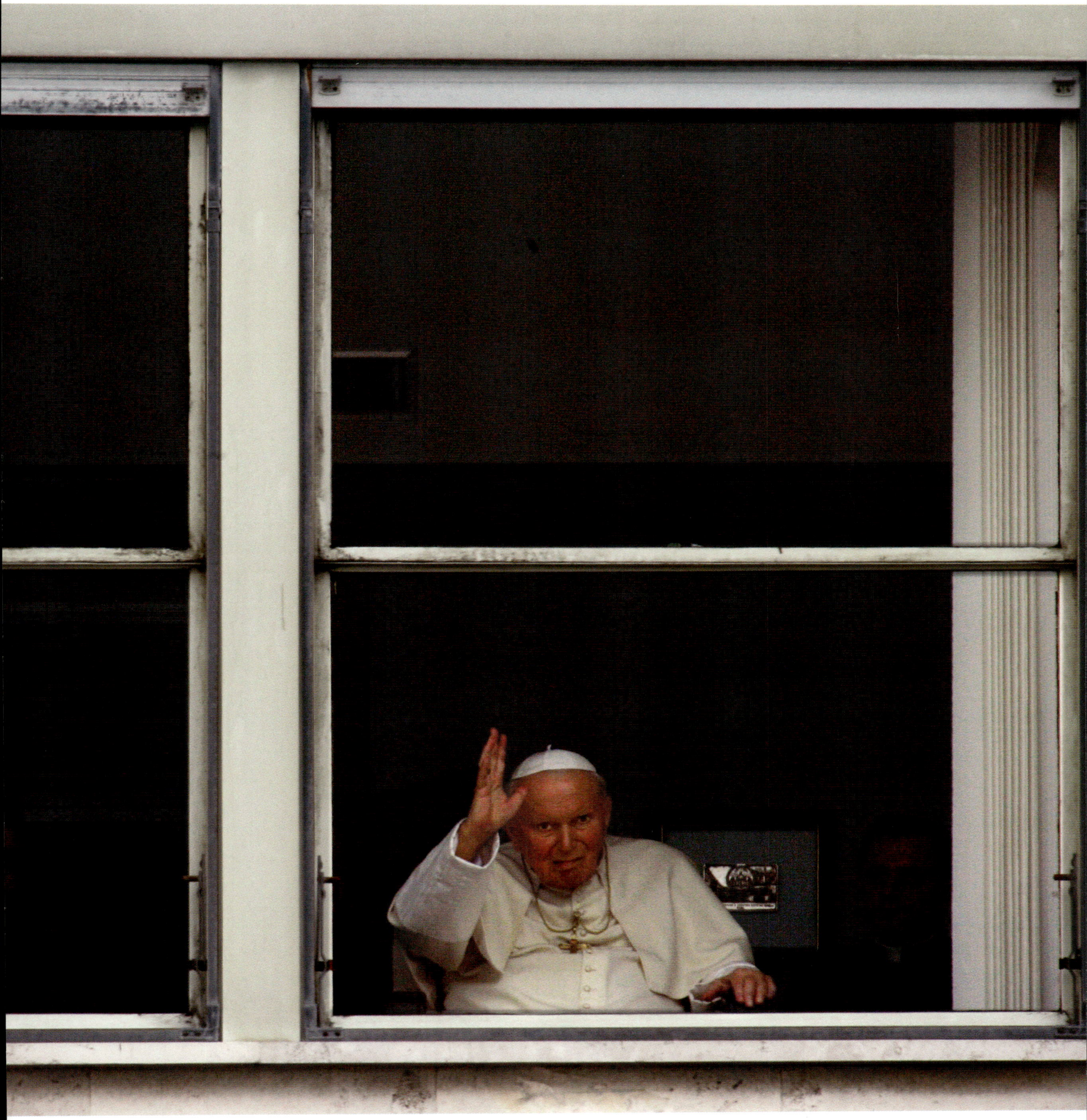

208 and 208-209 Rome, February 2005 – John Paul II leaves the Gemelli Hospital, where he was admitted during a bout of flu. This was the second of the two hospital stays that were to take place that month.

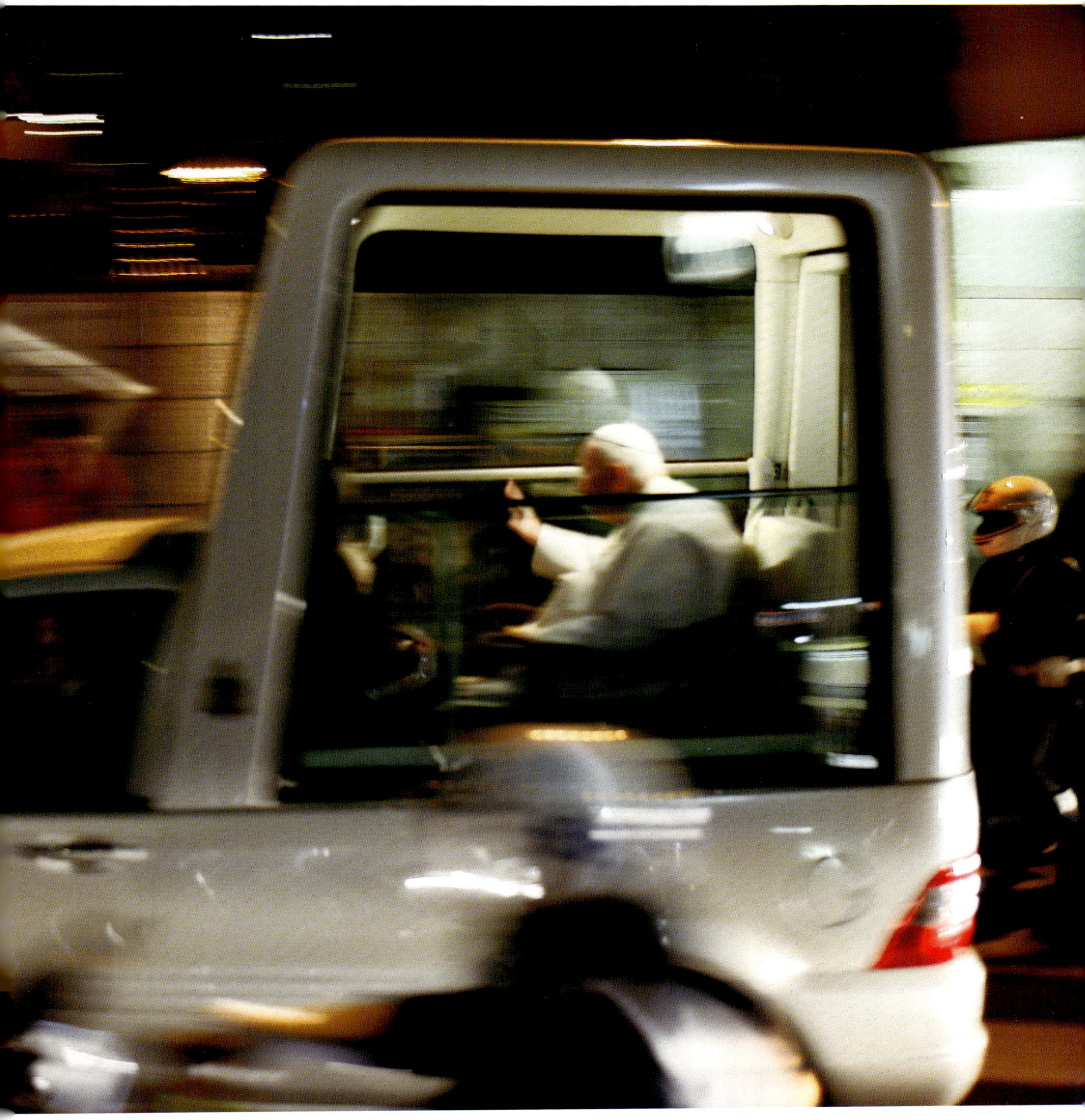

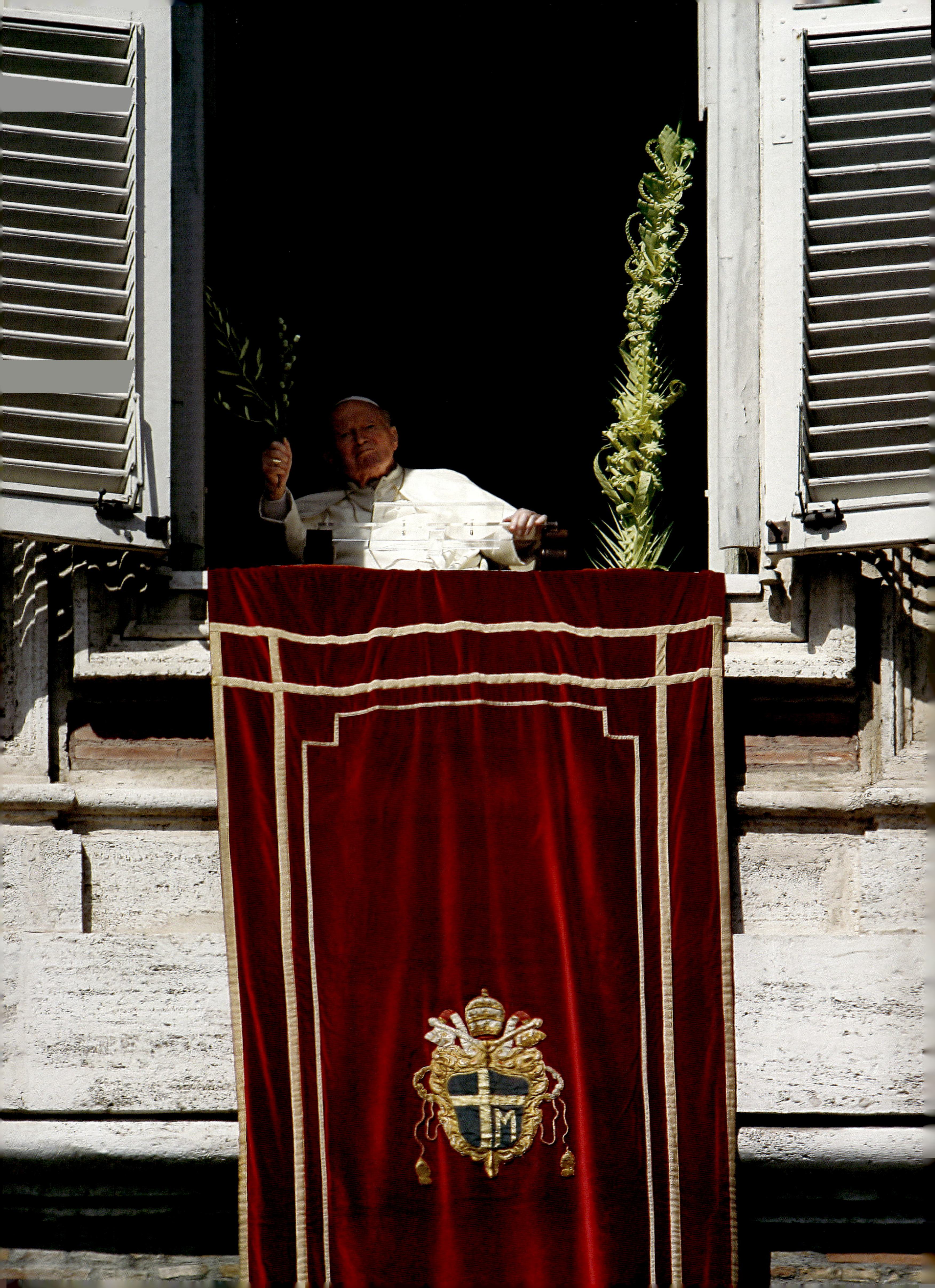

210 *Vatican City, March 20th, 2005* – *John Paul, who is visibly tired and in pain, nevertheless appears briefly at the window of his private apartment to bless the thousands of pilgrims who are waiting to catch a glimpse of him in St. Peter's Square on Palm Sunday.*

211 *Vatican City, March 30th, 2005* – *The moment in which John Paul II attempts to speak is heartrending. He makes a huge effort but his voice will not sound. Only with his hands, and with his features cloaked in weariness, was he able to deliver a blessing for the Wednesday General Audience: this was to be his last public appearance.*

212-213 *Vatican City, April 5th, 2005* – *The body of John Paul II lies in state for three days in St. Peter's Basilica, beneath the High Altar, where hundreds of thousands of faithful come to pay homage.*

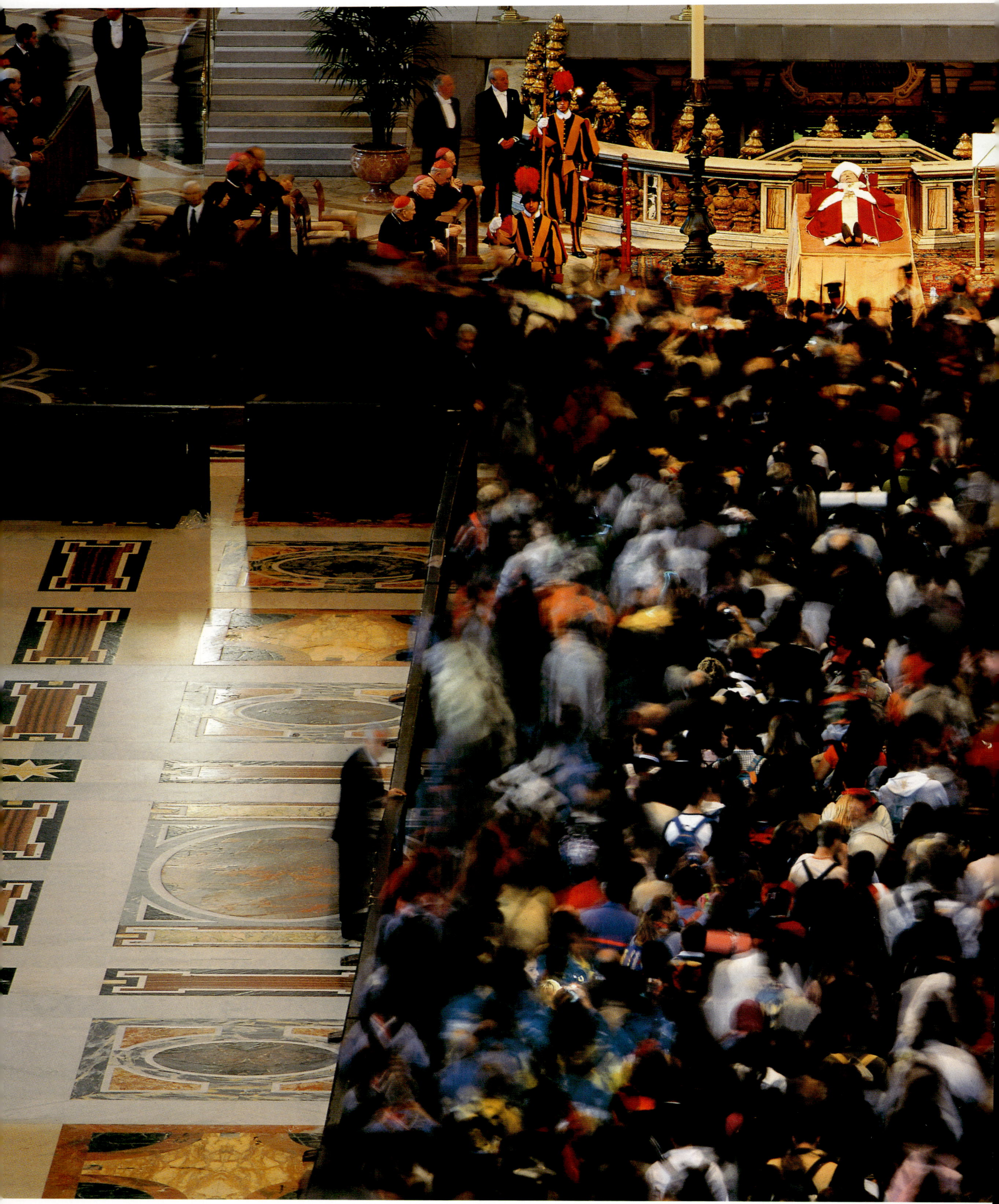

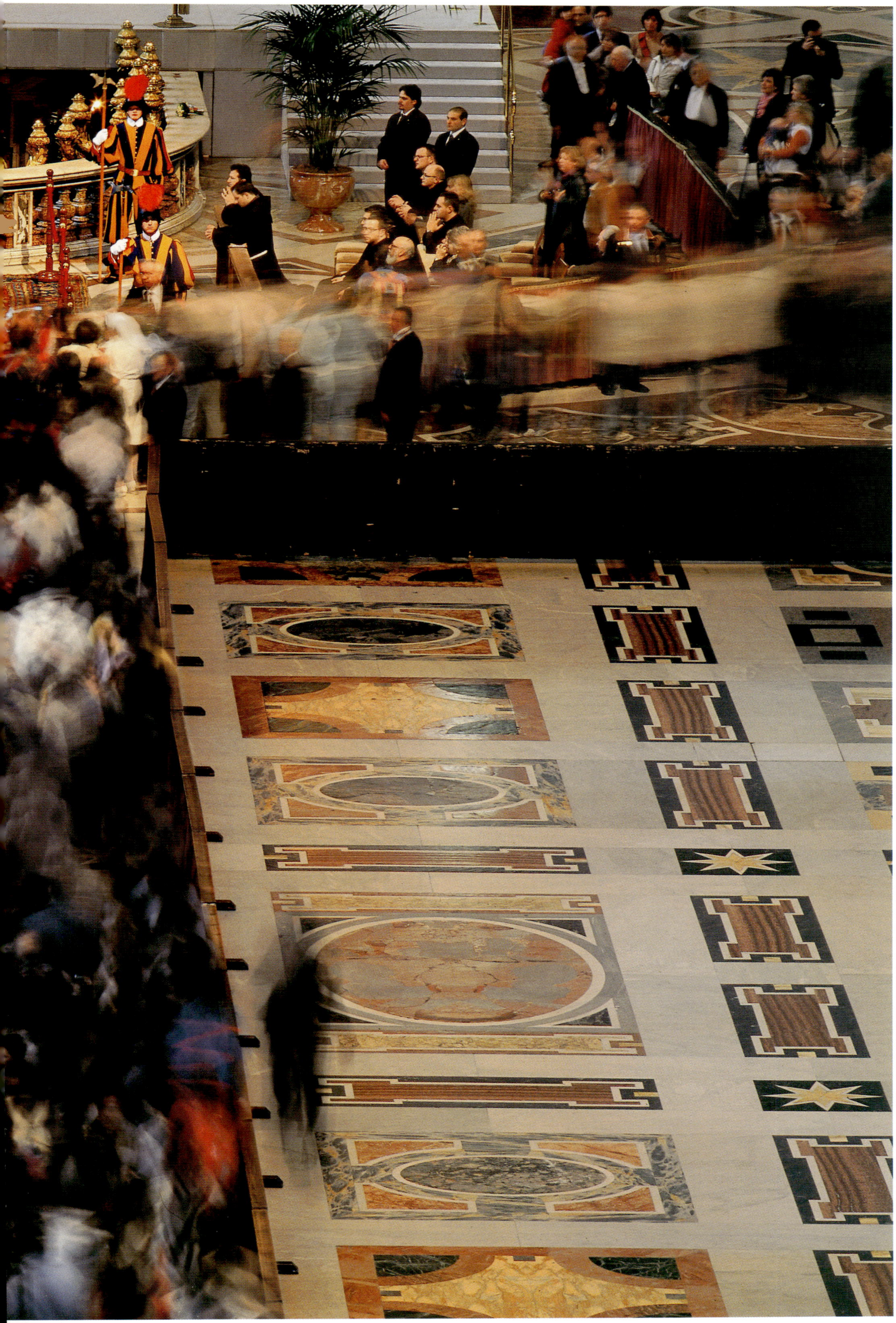

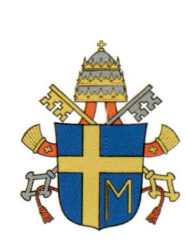

214 Vatican City, April 2nd, 2005 – The faithful have been worried for two days, waiting to hear news about the Pope's state of health; this is the moment in which they learn that Karol Wojtyla, "the Polish Pope" has died.

214-215 Vatican City, April 6th, 2005 – More than two million pilgrims queued for an average of 12-14 hours to pay their respects to the body of John Paul II: the faithful, most of whom were young people, spent the night queuing or sleeping, with the help of the Civil Defence authorities, in and around St. Peter's Square.

216 and 217 Vatican City, April 4th, 2005 – The transfer: with a solemn, moving procession, the pontiff's body, carried by twelve pall bearers and escorted by the Swiss Guards, is transferred into St. Peter's Basilica.

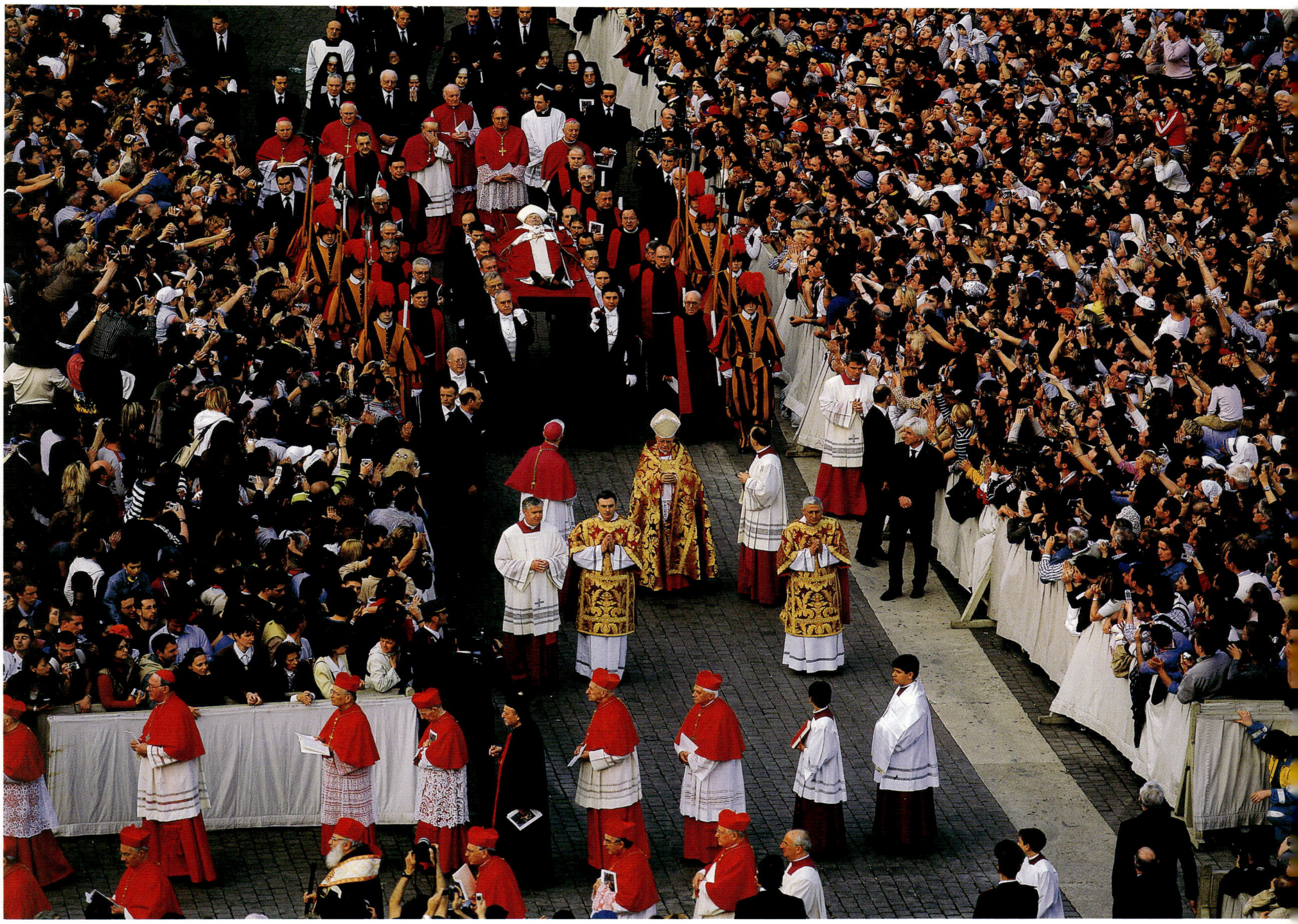

218

218-219 and 219 Vatican City, April 8th, 2005. Some 200 heads of state came to Rome to the solemn funeral of Pope John Paul II. President Ciampi of Italy and his wife Franca, moved and deeply saddened, and the King Baudouin and Queen Paula of Belgium, say goodbye to the simple cypress coffin for the last time, as it is carried away by the pall bearers. On the left, George W. Bush, Condoleeza Rice and Bill Clinton can be seen. In the front row (on the right), King Juan Carlos and Queen Sofia of Spain (right), and King Abdullah and Queen Rania of Jordan (left) bow as the coffin is taken past.

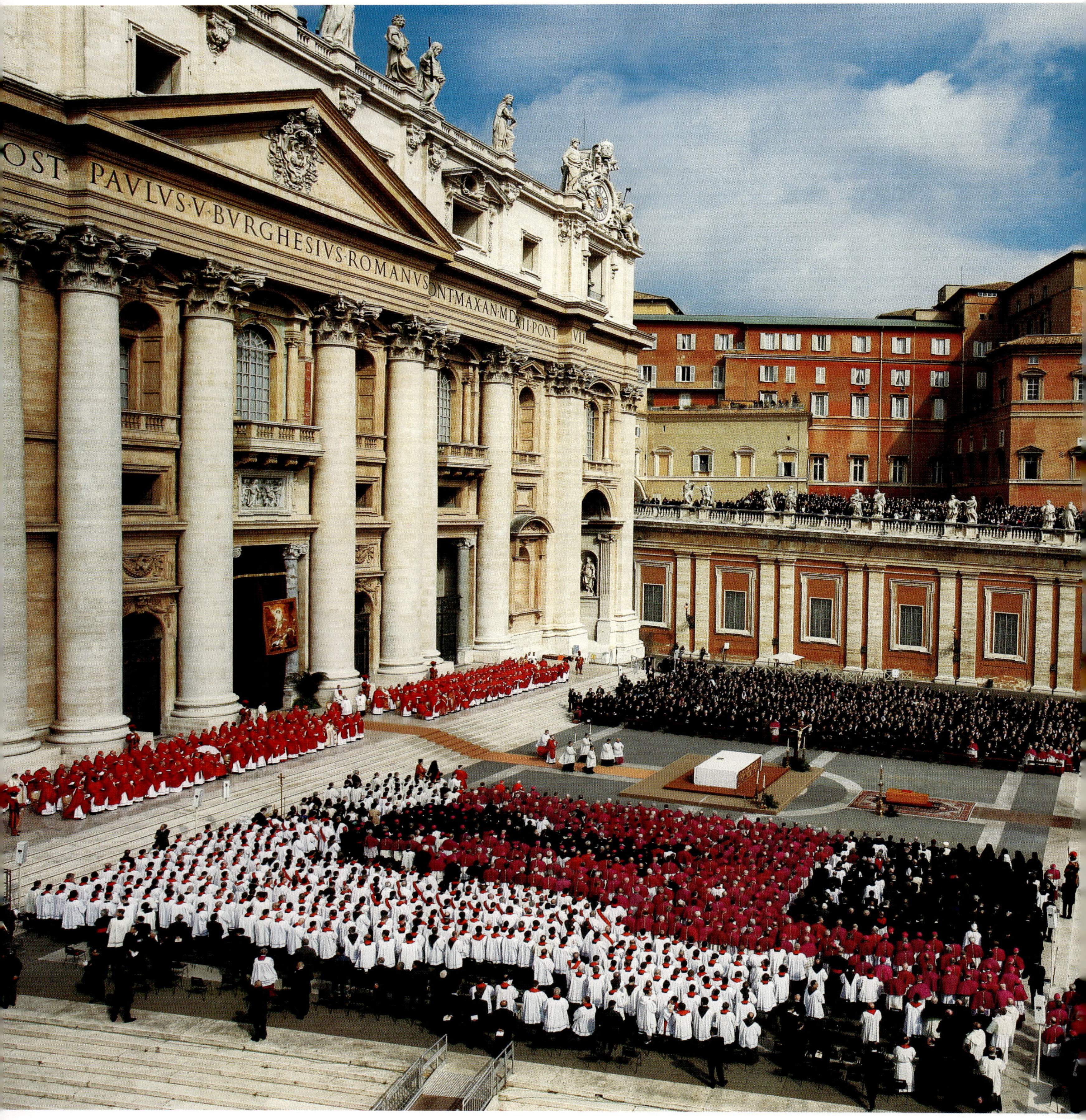
OST PAVLVS·V·BVRGHESIVS·ROMANVS
ONT·MAX·AN·MD XII·PONT VII

220-221 Vatican City, April 8th, 2005 – Cardinals, bishops and heads of state gather on the parvis of St. Peter's Basilica. The funeral ceremony was conducted by Cardinal Ratzinger, the future Pope Benedict XVI.

221 Vatican City, 8th April 8th, 2005 – The morning of the funeral rites is overcast and cloudy. The weather conditions seem to reflect the grief of the faithful. For several minutes the wind blows the pages of the Gospels placed on the coffin, as if to express a last message of hope and comfort from the Pope John Paul II.

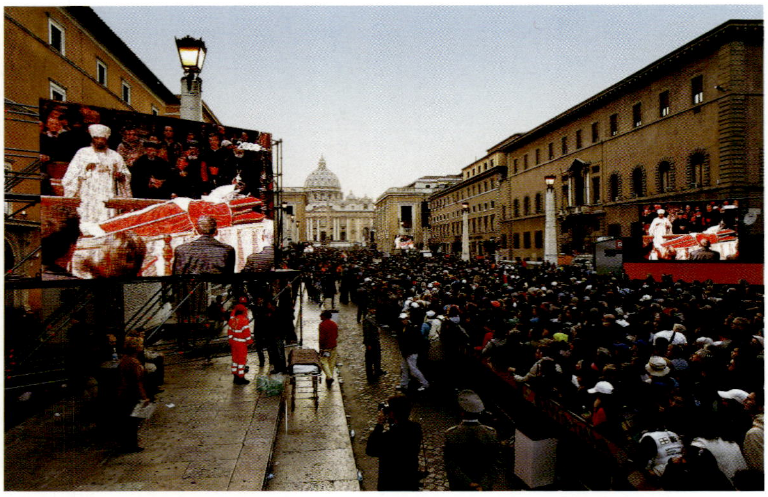

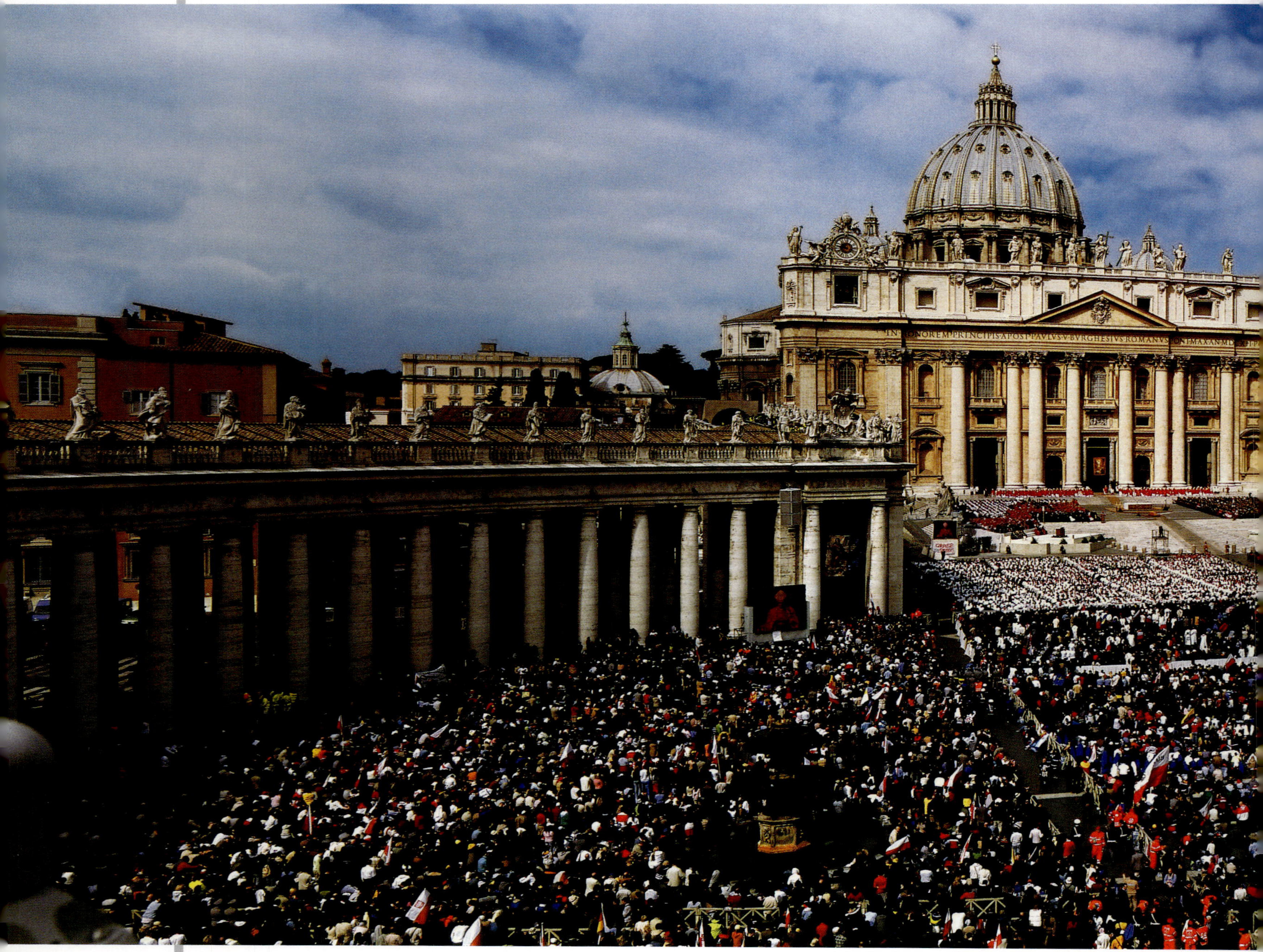

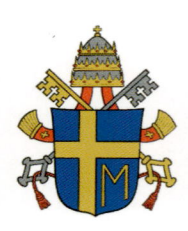

222 and 223 Vatican City, April 8th, 2005: Between St. Peter's Square and Via della Conciliazione, some 500,000 pilgrims tolerated fatigue, the heat of daytime and the cold of night, the hours of waiting in line to attend the funeral and say their goodbyes to the Polish Pope, Jean Paul II the Great, as Cardinal Ratzinger called him during his homily, a "Santo Subito" (A Saint now!) as the crowds in the Square demanded on the day of the funeral itself.

The author and the photographer would like to thank the following people whose assistance made this book possible:

Biagio Agnes, Valentina Alazraki, Andrea Andermann, Riccardo Auci, Roberto Bettoni, Egildo Biocca, Raul Bonarelli, Don Giorgio Bruni, Camillo Cibin, Clara Colelli, Giuseppe D'Amico, Alessandro Di Napoli, Mons. Stanislao Dziwisz, Franco Fegatelli, Mons. John Patrick Foley, Alberto Gasparri, Suor Giovanna Gentili, Dott. Domenico Giani, Giancarlo Giuliani, Angelo Gugel, Hubert Henrotte, Padre Federico Lombardi, Arturo Mari, Chiara Mariani, Mons. Piero Marini, Alain Mingam, Joaquin Navarro-Valls, Michele Neri, Franco Origlia, Mons. Pierfranco Pastore, Laura Riccioni, Padre Leonardo Sapienza, Angelo Scelzo, Francesco Sforza, Vittorio Storaro, Roberto Tucci, Vik Van Brantegem, Marjorie Weeke

A special thanks to Ada Masella

All photographs in this book are by Gianni Giansanti. www.giansanti.com
except for the followings: pages 176-177 Arturo Mari / Osservatore Romano;
page 144 AP Photo/Mark Lennihan; pages 2-3, 8-9 Catholic Press Photo.